SEE IT.
SAY IT.
APPRECIATE IT!

THE MANAGER'S GUIDE TO EMPLOYEE RECOGNITION

DEBRA COREY

First published in Great Britain as a softback original in 2022

Copyright © Debra Corey

The moral right of this author has been asserted.

Cover designed by Leonie Williamson

Edited by Chloe Thompson

Typesetting and publishing by UK Book Publishing
www.ukbookpublishing.com

ISBN: 978-1-915338-61-7

Contents

Foreword 1

Introduction 4

Chapter 1:
The Superpowers of Recognition.. 12

Chapter 2:
See it. Say it. Appreciate it! 29

Chapter 3:
Your Recognition Toolkit.. 38

Chapter 4:
The Four Golden Rules of Appreciation 56

Chapter 5:
Rule 1 – Make Recognition Meaningful................................ 61

Chapter 6:
Rule 2 – Make Recognition Unified 73

Chapter 7:
Rule 3 – Spotlight Your Recognition.................................... 83

Chapter 8:
Rule 4 – Make Recognition Timely....................................... 89

Chapter 9:
Next Steps 99

Conclusion 108

References 110

Appendix 1:
Formal Recognition Examples 112

Appendix 2:
Sample Recognition Messages 116

Appendix 3:
Recognition Planning Worksheet 118

FOREWORD

I'm pleased to share with you a foreword that was written by a manager, my wonderful husband, Ken Corey. I am in awe of how he has embraced recognition and made it work for him and for his people, which is why I asked him to explain the journey he's been on to get here, and how he's used and continues to use appreciation through recognition as an effective and meaningful management tool. I hope you find his perspective as a manager helpful, relatable and inspirational.

A MANAGER'S RECOGNITION JOURNEY

As an engineer, I've often been skeptical about those corporate initiatives and programs that seemed to be busy work. You know the ones — things like performance management, values, and yes, even recognition. And why is that? Well, they didn't get the product out the door! They were always something we pulled out once a year, or maybe in "good" companies, once a month. Other than the occasional lip-service, as managers we never paid much attention to them as they didn't seem to make much difference to us on a day-to-day basis.

It's not that the initiatives were ill-intentioned or poorly designed, as managers we just didn't apply them in our regular day- to-day experiences, and never thought about them. In hindsight, I know that the key to success in recognition *is* to make it a part of your day-to-day routine ... so no wonder they didn't work! That colored my perception of them across the board.

I first saw the benefit of recognition when my lovely wife and I (the author of the book you're reading!) started adoption courses on our journey to adopt our two children. During the courses, part of our learnings were to understand how to show appreciation and recognition for our adopted children. We were told that "recognition must be detailed, specific, and concrete to have its desired effect." As a stay-at-home dad, I got to see the effect of praise not only on the children, but in how the teachers used it with parents, and how our friends used it for each other. I practiced using it whenever the opportunity arose.

After going back into the workforce, it became natural to be using recognition and these principles in the office. I loved the effect that it had on the people around me.

When I started leading a team at Santander, recognition helped me solve a lot of issues at work. Not just in praising the people below me in the hierarchy but those above me as well. When COVID-19 lockdowns first hit, we were separated and virtual. We struggled with how to maintain connections with one another, and didn't have any real solution in place. So to help, I created a #kudos channel in Microsoft Teams, and the response was gratifying. It was instant, in-the-moment, public, free praise that anyone could give to anyone else.

At the beginning, I was the only person posting. But as time went on, other leaders started posting. Finally, individuals realized they could post too, and that's when the channel came into its own. Our entire team came together and bonded in part because of that kudos channel. We could recognize when someone went above and beyond, and people could see what was going on, even if they weren't face to face. At Santander during the first lockdown there were so many great examples of people helping customers and their fellow colleagues through a difficult time, so it was a great tool to celebrate these moments.

When I moved to Curve as an engineering manager I created a similar channel in our internal communications. I'd learned a few lessons from my time at Santander: find cheerleaders to help spread the word, teach people to look for things to praise and bring senior leadership along to encourage the channel. By using these lessons the channel in Curve was even more effective.

What's the big deal? You could just say "Atta-boy" or "Atta-girl." Sure, the person being praised would feel good for a moment but that will fade quickly as they realize just how little effort you put into the praise.

Good recognition gets past imposter syndrome and can't be denied because it's specific. But that's not all it does. Recognition also reinforces good behavior, and teaches that behavior to the rest of the team. Even better, it prevents people from getting envious precisely because that moment of recognition is undeniable. There's no doubt that person went above and beyond, and we should be celebrating it. Finally, it builds trust. By celebrating good behavior, we're distributing credit across the whole organization, and more people feel like they might get a share of that credit. It bonds, builds, rewards, teaches and feels good to give.

Why don't more organizations do it (or at least do it effectively)? I have no idea, but do keep in mind this is not a once-and-done exercise. Every day you should be considering the examples in this book to see which might be useful in your situation and for your people.

Is recognizing hard? No. Anyone can do it for anyone else, it just takes starting. I'm proof of that!. This book will start you down the path to both give recognition and to ensure that recognition has the biggest impact possible.

Debra's wealth of experience has gone into shaping the suggestions in this book, and I've been thrilled to see her journey going from conception to final written form. I hope you benefit as much as I have from talking with Debra while she was working on this book and in reading the finished product.

Ken Corey – Senior Engineering Manager (and proud husband)

INTRODUCTION

There's a phrase that is commonly seen on public transport in the U.K. which is "See it. Say it. Sorted." Every time I see or hear it, I think to myself, what a great phrase. It's a call to action, encouraging and driving people to take personal ownership and responsibility, and at the same time, work together to overcome a problem and challenge.

As they say on the British Transport Police website: "We've all got a role to play in keeping the rail network safe, and we rely on you to be our eyes and ears."

I love this phrase so much that I've decided to create my own version, my own call to action that relates to the important topic of employee recognition. I've changed the third part of the phrase from "Sorted," which refers to the idea of handing the problem over to someone else, to "Appreciate it!"

This does two things:

- First, it makes the point that as a manager you need to **take personal ownership and responsibility throughout the recognition process** and not hand it off to someone else.
- And secondly, the process needs to **focus on showing appreciation**, doing so by looking for and appreciating your entire team's actions and behaviors through acts and moments of recognition.

With this in mind, my version of the website would say: "As managers, we all have a role to play in keeping our businesses safe and successful by making our people feel valued and appreciated. Together, we are the eyes, ears and mouths, capturing all of the moments that need and deserve to be appreciated through recognition."

THE MATH AND SCIENCE OF APPRECIATION

But why does it matter, why do we even *need* a call to action? We'll go into more detail shortly, but I thought it was important to tackle it from the start. So let me share how appreciation has statistically and scientifically been proven to motivate your people, improve their performance, drive business results and so much more.

Let's start with a piece of data from a study[1] that asked employees **what matters most to them**. The clear winner was appreciation, with 37% of respondents saying "recognize me," higher than getting more pay (7%), getting more training (6%) or getting a promotion (4%), showing how **appreciation matters the most to our people**.

The study also shows that **appreciation and recognition matter to our companies**, for when answering the question of what matters most to them, respondents also said that by getting more recognition, they'd **produce great work**. Two other studies found similar results, with one[2] reporting that 79% of employees said they'd **work harder** if their efforts were recognized, and another[3] reporting that 82% of employees said that praise and recognition are leading factors in helping them **improve their job performance**.

THE IMPACT OF RECOGNITION FROM A MANAGER

And since this book is for managers, let me share four more pieces of data to highlight the impact that recognition from *you, as a manager,* can have on your team and your company as a whole:

- **Stronger business results** – A study found that when leaders and managers are actively involved in employee recognition, companies are 9 times more likely to have strong business results[4].

- **Improved relationship with managers** – 58% of employees report that their relationship with their manager would improve if they were given more recognition[5].

- **Improved morale** – 70% of employees said that their motivation and morale would improve if their managers would simply thank them more[6].

- **Improved trust** – Employees who were recognized were 34% more likely to trust senior leaders and 33% more likely to trust managers, compared to those who had never been recognized[5].

- **More likely to recognize others** – When a manager recognizes their people, they in turn are 2.5 times more likely to recognize others[5].

A Little Thanks Goes a Long Way

A study was conducted at Wharton School at the University of Pennsylvania to examine the effects of gratitude on fundraisers' prosocial behaviors in raising money to benefit the university.

A group of 41 fundraisers was randomly divided into two groups. One group made phone calls to solicit alumni donations in the same way they always had, and the second group, who worked on a different day, received a pep talk from their director, telling them, "I am very grateful for your hard work. We sincerely appreciate your contributions to the university."

The results found that the expression of gratitude increased the number of calls by more than 50% for the week, while fundraisers who received no thanks made about the same number of calls as the previous week.

RECOGNITION RELEASES HAPPINESS CHEMICALS

Along with the math, believe it or not, there's also a science behind the power of appreciation. Without getting into too much detail, there's evidence showing that chemicals in our brain called "happiness chemicals" are released when we feel respected for the work we do and when we are praised. These chemicals — dopamine, serotonin and oxytocin, all influence how we feel, with sensations of happiness, closeness and joy, thus impacting how our body functions physically, mentally and emotionally.

Studies have shown that when you praise someone your words trigger their hypothalamus, which is the part of your brain that acts as your body's smart control coordinating center, having a key role to play in productivity. And that's because when the brain gets triggered to produce more of these chemicals through appreciation, they boost its work and your brain will work at its maximum to do its best.

To make this point when I run recognition workshops with managers, I normally hand out chocolates. And after giving them a moment to have a bite or two, I ask them how the chocolate made them feel, and the unanimous response is feelings of joy, feeling all warm and fuzzy. I then explain that the same happiness chemicals are released from your brain when eating chocolate as the ones released when recognition happens. And, the good news is that you don't have to work out to work off the calories from recognition!

FIVE KEY THEMES

Throughout this book I'll also be sharing a lot of strategies and tips to help you get recognition and appreciation "right," since I know from experience that this is not always an easy thing to do. To give you an idea of what you'll see in my book, I've pulled together five key themes that I strongly believe help you get and stay on the "right" path:

1. We need to **focus on the feeling of appreciation**, doing it in a way that is meaningful for our employees and to our company. It doesn't start with a fancy trophy, a beautiful gift or even money. It starts with a feeling that our people matter, that they make a difference, that they're seen, that they belong, and that they're appreciated for who they are and what they've done.

2. We need to have an **inclusive approach** to recognition, one where everyone is invited to the party, where we're all treated as individuals and which drives a sense of belonging through appreciation.

3. We need to **recognize the small inputs and contributions** that lead and add up to the ultimate outcome, and which keep our people and our work on track and in focus.

4. We need to **remove the "winner versus loser" mentality** that is often seen when we recognize only a few top people and ignore others that are also contributing to the business, thus changing recognition from a motivator to a demotivator.

5. We need to **remove the constraints and guard rails** that we've built into when and how we recognize our people, giving it more freely in a continuous and timely manner.

People will forget what you said. People will forget what you did. But people will never forget how you made them feel.

MAYA ANGELOU

GETTING STARTED

I hope that what I've said so far has piqued your interest, and you're ready to learn how you can master the skills of appreciation and recognition. Here are four things to keep in mind as you get started:

1. **We need to move away from the ways of traditional recognition** – Throughout the book you'll notice that many of my suggestions and tips challenge traditional ways of recognizing our people, moving away from them and into new ways. My reason for this is because, to put it bluntly, *many no longer work*! Given all of the changes in the workplace and our workforces, they no longer meet the needs of our businesses and people. I encourage you to be open-minded, embracing the new ways and letting go of those that may be holding you back as you go forward.

We have a long way to go to make our people feel appreciated

Too many employees are not being recognized, with one survey finding that almost seven out of 10 (65%) employees have not been appreciated in the last year[7]. And no surprise, this large percentage of the workforce says that they don't feel appreciated. This needs to change!

---

2. **Much of what we need to do we learned when we were children** – In a previous book, where I wrote about challenging the ways we engage our people, I said that "maybe we've forgotten what we learned as children." This is definitely true when it comes to recognition. If we go back to these childhood lessons, we were told to say thank you, to be grateful, and that it's the thought that counts, not the gift. It's key to keep these in mind in our new ways of recognizing people and meeting our goal of making them feel appreciated. They are even more important now as adults in the workplace.

3. **You need to find your own recognition style** – I will be sharing lots of strategies and tips throughout the book. Some you will agree with and some you may not. And do you know what? That's absolutely fine. I'm a big believer that in order for something to work and to be "right" it needs to be right for you. You need to find your own style when it comes to recognition, something that feels comfortable and genuine to you.

   Later I'll share a story about a colleague who used to give his employees a bag of homemade chocolate chip cookies to thank them, which is great for him, but it may not feel right to you. I suggest that as you go through the book you highlight those that "speak" to you, and then use them, along with your own unique (and I'm sure amazing) ideas, to find and develop your own recognition style.

4. **Use the book as a guide** – And finally, let me say that this book is not a textbook, it is not a reference book, it is a guide. This means that it has a bias for action, giving you not just theory and data, but practical and actionable strategies, approaches, techniques and tips to guide and support you to get things done. Pick and choose those that work best to help you create and drive an appreciation and recognition culture with your team and at your company. To help you with this, each chapter ends with a "call to action" section so you can start driving change right away. Each chapter also has an inspirational quote because, well, I do love a good quote!

So let's get started . . .

CHAPTER 1:
The Superpowers of Recognition

CHAPTER OBJECTIVES

In this chapter we'll cover:

- How recognition can turn our employees into superheroes, helping them feel and perform at their best.

- How recognition can help and contribute towards your team and your company's success.

- How recognition can have a ripple effect on those that give, receive and see it.

- What's holding us back from showing appreciation.

INTRODUCTION

We all love superheroes, right? After all, they possess supernatural or superhuman powers to do things better than mere mortals, and, just as important, can use these powers to fight evil and protect us from supervillains. In the business world, these supervillains are external forces and at times, our competitors.

But that's just in comic books and movies, certainly we don't have superheroes in the real world, and certainly not in the workplace, right? Wrong! I've seen employees turn into superheroes countless times, doing extraordinary things to help their companies innovate more, succeed more, and overcome obstacles and challenges.

And the good news is that one of the tools that we as managers can use to turn our "normal" people into superheroes is, you guessed it, **appreciation and recognition**. Now your employees may not turn into the kind of superheroes that are able to leap tall buildings or lift a bus, but the superpowers derived from recognition have been proven to help your employees feel and be at their best, which is good for them and for your company.

The great thing about recognition is that all employees, regardless of who they are and the job they perform, have the opportunity and potential to be superheroes. It's not limited to someone at a specific level or job function, or a person with a certain number of years with the company, recognition can (and should) bring out the superhero in all of us!

RECOGNITION SUPERPOWERS

In this chapter we'll be exploring 10 superpowers ignited by appreciation and recognition. As you'll see, the list is quite extensive both in what they are and the difference and impact they can make – to your people, to you and to your business. I'd explain them all in detail, but at a high level, here are the 10 areas where recognition and appreciation can deliver power to your company and people:

Employee engagement	Belonging	Happiness	Wellbeing	Burnout
Trust	Awareness	Productivity	Business results	Retention

" There's a superhero in all of us. By showing appreciation we're empowering our people to put on their superhero capes, setting them free to be their best and to help defeat the supervillains. "

Superpower #1: Employees are more engaged

Let's start with employee engagement, something that most companies focus on and measure as they've come to see the power it can have on their business. To show that it's not just fluffy business words, studies show the positive influence that high employee engagement can have on company sales, revenue, customer service, safety and turnover, to name a few, showing the true extent of its impact.

Engaged versus disengaged, what's the difference?

There are lots of ways to define what an engaged employee is. A common definition is that they're employees who are involved in, enthusiastic about, and committed to their work and workplace, or that they care about their work and about the performance of the company, and they want to feel that their efforts could make a difference.

But to fully understand this term, let me ask you to flip it around and think about what a *disengaged* employee is. Think of someone who doesn't care about their work, so they're being sloppy and making mistakes. Think of someone who puts such little effort into what they do that they slow themselves and others down, being less productive. Or think of someone who doesn't speak up when they see a problem, or better yet, an opportunity to do things differently or a new idea to help your business succeed. These are disengaged employees, and these are the ones that can put you and your business at risk.

Recognition has been proven to be a key driver of employee engagement, with a study by Deloitte[8] finding that **employee engagement was 14% higher** in organizations where they practice employee recognition than in those without recognition. This should come as no surprise, for a key driver for engagement is to feel valued, which is a direct result of recognition.

Superpower #2: Employees have a better sense of belonging

It's been proven that one of the biggest contributors to employee engagement is a sense of belonging, something that can only happen when there is a shared sense of purpose, feeling fully accepted, and where employees genuinely care about one another and have a willingness to invest emotional energy for the benefit of each other. Recognition can be a key contributor to this sense of belonging, with each recognition act you give showing your people that they're accepted, cared about for who they are and what they've done, and worthy of their recognition efforts.

One study[9] goes on to show that employees with a strong sense of belonging are over **six times more likely to be engaged** than those who don't, and **12% happier.** And another[10] study found that if employees feel like they belong, companies reap substantial bottom-line benefits such as a **56% increase in job performance**, a **50% drop in turnover**, and a **75% reduction in sick days**. And to bring this to life, the report shows that for a 10,000-person company, this would result in annual savings of more than $52 million.

Superpower #3: Employees are happier

Employee happiness, like employee engagement, can also have a positive impact on a business. In Shawn Achor's book *The Happiness Advantage,* he talks about how happiness leads to employees who feel more positive, are more creative, are better at solving problems, and are more effective collaborators, all of which contribute to a more successful company.

And what is that connection to recognition? Well, according to a study[11] that ranked the 26 factors of happiness on the job, they found that "the most important single job element for all people is appreciation for their work," which, as we know, occurs through recognition.

The reason for this is partly down to fulfilling basic human needs, but also down to science. As explained in the introduction, "happiness chemicals" are released when you are recognized. This means that by recognizing someone you are giving them the gift of happiness, which, as gifts go, is a pretty great one!

Superpower #4: Employees have better overall wellbeing

Related to happiness, and something new that I added to my list during the COVID-19 pandemic, is the impact that recognition can have on wellbeing. We've seen that in a world filled with uncertainty and challenges, recognition was used as a way to give hope and strength to our workforces, lifting their spirits and helping them be more resilient. As businesses and their workforces continue to face everyday challenges, recognition can and will be a way to support overall wellbeing objectives.

Superpower #5: Employees are less burned out

When an employee's wellbeing is not taken care of, they're often at risk for burnout, which according to the World Health Organization happens when we feel 1) depleted or exhausted, 2) mentally distant from our job or have negative feelings or cynicism about our job, and 3) reduced professional efficacy. The impact of this, according to a study by Gallup[12], is that employees who say they very often or always experience burnout at work are:

- 63% more likely to take a sick day.
- 2.6 times more likely to be actively seeking a different job.
- 13% less confident in their performance.

And since burnout is increasingly on the rise due to symptoms of the more fast-paced, complex and demanding modern workplace, which also has made technology blur the lines between home life and work life, it's something that we all need to take seriously.

Recognition can contribute to preventing and/or reducing burnout as it addresses some of the factors that can lead to it such as feelings of unfair treatment at work, unclear communication from managers and lack of manager support. Supporting this, one study[13] found that when recognition hits the mark, **73% of employees are less likely to always or very often feel burned out.**

A little recognition can provide a morale boost

To better understand the effectiveness of symbolic recognition for public sector employees, a study was run to look at the impact of sending social workers personalized letters of appreciation to their home addresses. They randomly assigned for half of the social workers to receive letters from their direct managers, while the other half did not receive a letter.

The letters contained two sentences of positive feedback. The first sentence was selected from a menu of options such as, "your work has consistently had a positive impact on the children you work with," and "your continued dedication and hard work make children and families in the region better off every day," and the second sentence was written by the manager themselves. In this way, they ensured that the letters were reasonably standardized but still personalized.

One month after this simple intervention, the social workers who received a letter reported feeling significantly more valued, more recognized for their work, and more supported by their organization than those who didn't receive a letter. There were also positive (though not quite statistically significant) impacts on subjective wellbeing, belonging, intrinsic motivation and sickness absence rates for social workers who received letters.

Superpower #6: Employees are more trusting

Employee trust is another factor that has been proven to have a positive impact on the success of a company. From productivity to innovation, companies with high levels of trust have been found to outperform those with low levels of trust.

And again, recognition has an important part to play, with a study[2] saying that one of the most effective ways of building trust for managers and senior leaders is through frequent recognition. The study found that employees who were recognized were 34% more likely to trust senior leaders and 33% more likely to trust managers, compared to those who had never been recognized.

> **Recognition can lower levels of stress**
>
> A study[14] found that there was a 23% reduction in the stress hormone cortisol after appreciation was given, thus suggesting that an "attitude of gratitude" can lower your levels of stress, making you more resilient and able to handle the stressors and challenges that employees often face.

Superpower #7: Employees have a better sense of awareness

This next superpower moves from how the employee *feels* as a result of being recognized, to *what they receive:* An increased sense of awareness. This happens through feedback, which is formally and informally given each and every time an employee is recognized. It lets them know which of their efforts are most appreciated and valued, giving them a sense of achievement and an awareness of which actions and behaviors they should continue to lead to greater success. It also adds additional levels to feedback, moving it from binary – good or bad – to demonstrating differing levels of good within more situations.

Feedback through recognition quiets the negatives that take up so much of our employees' thoughts and time, helping them know that they're on the right track, that what they do matters and is truly making a difference.

According to a paper[15] by Gallup, "Recognition helps individuals accurately assess their performance. It provides the data we need to master new tasks and demands. It creates positive emotions, inspires broader perspectives and stimulates creative thinking – all at the foundation of innovation."

Feedback through recognition is like sending your employees on a free development course, giving them insights into how they're doing and how to develop their current and future skills.

And it's not just that one employee who becomes more aware because of recognition and benefits from insights. When you praise one member of your team, others learn that this is a desired behavior, showing them what good or great looks like.

Superpower #8: Employees are more productive

As shown in the previous data, it's not just employees who benefit from recognition, the company does as well. One way is through an increase in productivity, since having employees who are engaged, happy, trusting, aware and connected naturally leads to a more productive work environment. Recognition is a simple way to highlight what good and great look like in a business, leading to improved productivity as more and more employees mirror these behaviors.

A study[15] shows that **79% of employees would work harder** if they felt their efforts were being recognized, and research[16] done by Shawn Achor shows that **employee productivity can increase by 30%** when employees receive just one piece of praise a day.

And it's not just the receiver of recognition that is more productive. According to Achor, people who provide "social support" (which includes praising the actions of others) were **10 times more likely to be productive** than peers who didn't praise as often. As an added bonus, they were also more likely to be promoted.

People respond to praise, even from a robot

A study was conducted at a New York state hospital to increase the frequency by which hospital employees washed their hands as this was deemed extremely important for preventing the spread of disease. After warning signs and live video monitors were placed by hand sanitizer stations, only 10% of hospital employees were washing their hands. However, when an electronic board was placed in the hallway of the unit that gave employees instant feedback when they washed their hands, displaying a positive message such as "Good job!", the rate of compliance rose to 90% within four weeks.

The study shows the power of our need to be praised for good behavior, even when it's from an electronic robot!

Superpower #9: Company has stronger business results

Next, and something that should not be a surprise, is that these impacts will ultimately help your company be more successful and achieve higher business results.

According to a study[17], companies that excel at employee recognition on average are **12 times more likely to generate strong business results** than their peers. And to make it even more compelling, according to another report[7], if organizations would double the number of employees who receive recognition for their work on a weekly basis, they would experience a **24% improvement in quality** and a **10% reduction in shrinkage**, both which contribute to achieving company goals.

> **Gratitude has the power to energize**
>
> Some leaders think it is necessary to withhold positive sentiments at times in order to keep pressure on team members. But in reality, that pressure is likely to increase anxiety, which will then undermine productivity.
>
> In comparison, research from Robert Emmons of the University of California, Davis, shows that a leader who is more grateful amid difficult circumstances can help people cope.
>
> As he explains, "In the face of demoralization, gratitude has the power to energize. In the face of brokenness, gratitude has the power to heal. In the face of despair, gratitude has the power to bring hope."
>
> *Leading with Gratitude*, by Adrian Gostick and Chester Elton

Superpower #10: Company has better employee retention

And finally, recognition can have an impact on employee turnover, with employees staying longer because they feel valued and appreciated through recognition. We often believe that pay is the number one reason people leave a company, but in fact, a study[6] found that **79% of employees who quit their job cited a lack of recognition as the key driver**.

And for those who have not left their company, a study[15] found that employees who do not feel adequately recognized are **twice as likely to say they'll quit in the next year**.

And to put this in a financial context, according to one study, creating a culture of recognition can save a 10,000-employee company up to $16.1 million in turnover costs annually.

Do you want to lose your best performers?

A study was published in January 2022 by MIT Sloan on the "Great Resignation," revealing the top predictors of attrition and actions that managers can take in the short term to reduce it. One of the predictors listed was the failure to recognize performance, finding that it was **2.9 times more likely to contribute to attrition than compensation.**

It went on to state that high-performing employees are the "most likely to resent a lack of recognition for their results." This means that companies that are not focusing on recognition may be losing some of their most productive workers, especially in times of high turnover.

THE RIPPLE EFFECTS OF RECOGNITION

Let me add one more positive effect of recognition that is not a superpower, but rather a superpower accelerator. It's called the "ripple effect," and it happens when employees *receive*, *give* and even *see* recognition being given to colleagues. In psychology, they call this the "emotional contagion in groups," which talks about how moods, emotions and actions are transferred within groups.

Think of it like a giant game of tag, with one employee tagging another through recognition, and then another and then another. Each moment ignites and sparks the recognition superpowers with every tag.

Here are three ways this ripple effect happens through recognition:

1. The first has to do with giving more recognition after receiving it yourself. According to a study[6], employees who are recognized are **three times more likely to recognize someone else**, calling this "positive reciprocity," and creating a ripple or domino effect as more people are recognized, which turns into more people recognizing others, and so on and so on.

2. The next can be seen in companies where recognition is shared and celebrated socially, putting under the "spotlight" as I'll explain later in this guide. In these scenarios, there are two effects as a consequence of employees viewing the recognition messages. First, they can join in on the recognition by adding their own message and rippling and multiplying the effect it has on the receiver. Second, they can be inspired by the recognition to send out their own recognition message, rippling and multiplying the number of people receiving recognition.

3. And finally, there's an effect that I call "memory moments," which happens when we create memory moments through recognition that we experience when we receive it and also when we think back to it for years to come. I personally have many of these stored away in my mind and even my desk drawer, pulling them out every once in a while when I need a bit of a pick-me-up or a reminder of the value and impact that I've made.

RECOGNITION IS NOT A SILVER BULLET

Before I end, I thought it was important to make a point, which may be obvious, but still needs to be said. And that is that recognition on its own is not "a silver bullet" when it comes to achieving all of the things mentioned in this chapter. This means that it is not, as the dictionary defines it, a "simple and seemingly magical solution to a complicated problem."

Recognition needs to sit and work alongside all of the other elements managers use to engage their people – *your* people. Whether that's communicating to them in an open and honest way to build and maintain trust and connection, providing them development and growth opportunities or how you'll support their overall wellbeing, it's your responsibility to own recognition along with these other elements.

And if recognition has a shared responsibility within these other elements, recognition must also have a shared responsibility within your people. They need to take some personal ownership over it, using self-motivation to drive them to make better and more frequent contributions, and equally important, highlight these to you as their manager. I always challenge my people with this, saying that they can't expect me to see everything, and that although sometimes it can be uncomfortable to do so, they need to think like a marketer and market how they are contributing in their day-to-day work.

WHAT'S HOLDING MANAGERS BACK?

Let me end this chapter by asking an important question that must be addressed before we move on, and that is – what is holding managers (and possibly you) back from giving recognition and showing appreciation? In my experience, it is often one or more of the following seven reasons. And because I truly believe recognition and appreciation *are* so important, you'll find that none of these reasons are good enough for me to tell you that you don't have to recognize! I encourage you to take a few minutes to think through which of these apply to you, and thus what you need to do to change your mindset and approach to recognition.

Reason #1: I don't believe that recognition is important

As shared throughout this chapter, recognition and appreciation can and does deliver amazing positive results to the company, to your people, and to you as a manager. The data doesn't lie, it can truly make a difference in all of the ways shared previously, and thus it is important and critical to you and your business.

Reason #2: I don't believe recognition is my responsibility

A key part of your job as a manager is to show support and care for your people, helping them be their best, and showing them that you value them and their contributions. And, because recognition and appreciation are tools to help you do this, then it is *absolutely* your responsibility to do so.

Reason #3: I don't have the time for recognition

Let me say that yes, it does take time to give recognition. However, often it can take less than a minute or two to do so, which for something so important, you should be able to find time in your day. Also, consider the risk of not showing appreciation, with the negative consequences far outweighing the time you put into it.

Reason #4: I don't have the money for recognition

Recognition does not need to cost a lot of money, in fact, some of the most meaningful and effective recognition costs absolutely nothing. In Chapter 3 I'll share lots of tips and examples to bring this point to life, showing that recognition can be done on "the cheap" to make your people feel appreciated.

Reason #5: I don't have the skills

It is common to avoid things that you feel that you are not good at. But that is actually one of the main reasons that I wrote this guide, so that every manager has the skills and confidence to recognize their people. And because it is a skill, as I write about in Chapter 9, you need to practice it to make it become a habit.

Reason #6: I don't see opportunities to recognize

The next reason addresses a fundamental pitfall that I see many managers fall into, which is not being able to see or find opportunities to recognize. One of the reasons that this happens is because too often we focus on what's not working, losing sight of the good that is happening around us, and missing out on important opportunities to recognize others. There's a concept used in organizational psychology called the "appreciative inquiry," which is a strengths-based approach that focuses on searching for the best in our people. If, as I'll talk more about in Chapter 2, we look for and "see" the good, the recognition opportunities will more readily present themselves.

Reason #7: It's not important to me personally

Let me end with a reason that is often shared with me when I do recognition workshops, and that is that since recognition is not important to me, then it must not be important to my people. The simple response to this is that we are all different, and although yes, some people may not feel that they need to be recognized, many, actually the majority, actually do. Especially with our workforces being made up of higher percentages of younger employees, where showing appreciation is not a nice to do, but is essential to them, it is important to not use personal preferences as a blocker to recognizing others.

"Sometimes managers wrongly see recognition as a 'tip,' believing that it doesn't need to be given as employees are already being paid to do their job. We need to challenge this so that everyone is valued for the work that they do. After all, if you don't provide recognition, your competitors will!"

Judith Germain, Leadership Catalyst, The Maverick Paradox

Calls to action:

- Go back and review the list of the 10 recognition superpowers, highlighting those you believe are the most important to you as a manager and to your company (e.g. will help you meet your goals and objectives).

- Once highlighted, list in priority order (high to low) which are the most important. This will help you later as you start developing your recognition plans and ideas.

- Go back and review the list of the seven reasons for holding back on recognition, and jot down any that you believe apply to you so that you can come up with a plan to overcome these obstacles and roadblocks.

CHAPTER 2:
See it. Say it. Appreciate it!

CHAPTER OBJECTIVES

In this chapter we'll cover:

- Why and how a mantra can help create your recognition call to action.
- How to use the mantra to help you achieve your recognition objectives.

INTRODUCTION

Now that I've shared the many superpowers of appreciation and recognition, you're probably thinking to yourself – great, what can *I* do to release them in my people? In the next few chapters I'll be sharing specific tools, guiding principles, tips and next steps you can take, but first I wanted to share with you what I'm calling your "recognition mantra," your call to action. You may recognize it.

The mantra is "See it. Say it. Appreciate it!" which, as you well know, is also the title of this guide. I came up with it for these three reasons: First, because it highlights the actions we all need to take when it comes to appreciation and recognition, second, because it should be easy to remember, and thus used, and finally because it's a bit fun, and well, we all need a bit of fun in our lives, right?

A mantra is a word or phrase that's silently repeated and is often used to help keep focus and to get in the right frame of mind. The word "mantra" is actually derived from two Sanskrit roots; "manas," meaning "mind," and "tra," meaning "tool." I like this as it reminds me of other ways to think of and describe what a mantra is, and how it can be used.

When I was a competitive gymnast, I had a secret mantra that I'd say to myself before and during my practices and competitions to psych me up and keep me focused on successfully completing my moves and routines. It became so much of a part of me, that to this day I still use it in situations where I need positivity and motivation.

BRINGING YOUR MANTRA OUT TO PLAY

My hope is that you use this appreciation mantra going forward as a way to help you achieve your recognition and appreciation objectives, bringing it "out to play" as I like to think of it. To do this the right way, let me first share with you what the mantra means, and thus how it can help you create that focus, motivation and mindset.

See it – Look for recognition everywhere and anywhere

The first part of the mantra is "See it," as this is where it all begins. In training classes I often say that we all need to put our recognition "glasses" on, thus looking for and seeking out opportunities to recognize our people. This is absolutely critical, for if you don't first see the moments, then they will be missed, and the appreciation will never happen.

The absolute starting point of appreciation is to see it, to notice all of those moments that deserve to be recognized, to be intentional and take that first step.

I'm often asked by managers, what should I recognize, what warrants this action? The simple answer is (nearly) everything and anything, but since that isn't very helpful, here are eight examples to get you on your way:

- **Highlighting quality work** – When your employees stand out by putting time and effort into delivering quality work, it's cause for recognition. This shows them that you appreciate them doing what it takes to get things done.

- **Suggesting new ideas** – As you know, innovation is key to helping you and your company succeed, pushing the boundaries on what you do and how you get things done. Recognizing your people when they take the initiative to present a new idea can be a great way to thank them for this contribution, encouraging them and others to take this leap going forward.

- **Learning a new skill** – Key to the success of your people and your business is development, with these new skills key to helping them improve and be their best. To encourage this, it's important to recognize the achievement of these new skills, letting your people know that you value and appreciate them taking the time and putting the effort into this accomplishment.

- **Achieving key milestones** – It's important to recognize the achievement of key milestones, or what I like to call those "small wins." Doing so will help your employees feel valued for their contributions, and also energize them, giving them the boost and confidence they need to keep going to achieve their overall objectives.

- **Achieving outstanding results** – When your employees achieve outstanding results by delivering a major assignment or project, it's a perfect reason to recognize them. Use recognition as a cause for celebration, showing them the difference their contributions made in the final results.

- **Supporting a colleague or customer** – When one of your employees goes out of their way to support a colleague or customer, this is another opportunity to recognize them. By doing this, it shows them and others that providing this level of service is valued and important to you and to your company.

- **Showing teamwork and cooperation** – Look for opportunities to recognize not just individuals, but teams. When you see them working together and collaborating to deliver great work, use recognition as a way to celebrate and encourage new ways to break down silos within your business and get everyone working toward the same goals.

- **Living your company values** – And finally, just as important as the "what," so what your employees have accomplished, is the "how," or what many companies define as their company values or beliefs. These are the actions and behaviors that you have identified as the ones that you believe are essential in achieving your company's mission and purpose, and creating and maintaining the culture that is right for your business and people. And for this reason, recognizing employees for living your company values will send the message to them that they are important, encouraging them to live them over and over again.

Three rules of thumb

According to psychologist Dr. Hayley Lewis, there are three rules of thumb she uses when encouraging managers to look for recognition moments. These rules follow recognizing based on a combination of 1) Who they are, 2) The job that they do, and 3) The work that they've done. Some will surface more than others based on the person, their job and the situation, but all should be considered and used to recognize your people. Ultimately, this means there should always be something you can find to recognize.

At first, it may be difficult to see and find these recognition moments as you haven't been looking for them in the past, but trust me, it will get easier, and soon they'll "jump off the page" as they become so obvious and apparent.

What's key to this, and something I'll talk more about in Chapter 4, is doing it in a unified and inclusive way, "inviting everyone to the recognition party," as I often say. Think of it like putting on 3-D glasses, thus looking in many directions and dimensions to capture recognition moments from anyone and everyone.

Say it – Take action and make it happen

The next part of the mantra is "Say it," which means to say and do something once you see a moment that deserves to be recognized, taking action. Too often I hear managers say that they're too busy, that they don't have the time to do it, but as I always say in response, "Can you risk what happens if you don't do something?" or "Do you have the time to pick up the pieces if the person isn't recognized and fails to achieve the goals you've set for them, or worse, walks out the door?"

There are two components, two actions, that take place in this part of the mantra. The first is what you say in the **words** that you use to recognize your people. As I'm sure you've seen and felt, words can have a significant impact and power, which is why it's important to choose them wisely and get them right.

In Chapter 4 I'll be sharing with you a simple three-step model to help you craft a meaningful recognition message, getting the say right. Do take the time to read and practice this, using it to help you create the impact and lasting memory that your employee deserves and needs.

The other component is the action of **giving** the recognition. Sometimes it is just in words, in your message, and sometimes it is with some kind of reward. And as with words, getting it right is absolutely critical, for the wrong reward can deliver the wrong meaning and thus the wrong outcome. In the next chapter, I'll be sharing more detail on recognition tools that can be used for rewards, with five categories and lots of examples included to help you get it right.

Appreciate it! – Deliver the ultimate appreciation feeling

The last part of the mantra is "Appreciate it!" and is about delivering that appreciation feeling. What I mean by this is that throughout the recognition process it is important to focus on the end result that you are looking to achieve, which is that of well, appreciation. You want to make sure that all of the steps and actions you take get you to the goal you are trying to achieve, which is your employee genuinely feeling appreciated. If that feeling isn't met at the end of the day, you haven't met your objectives in delivering the recognition the right way.

Begin with the end in mind

In L. David Marquet's book titled *Turn the Ship Around!* he talks about the concept of beginning a task with the end in mind. He explains that as a Navy submarine captain "when you need to be at a certain spot in the ocean at a certain time to pick up a SEAL team - your operational planning starts with that endpoint location and time and you then imagine the problem backward to where you are now, planning the submarine's movements so that you end up where you need to be."

This is exactly what you need to do when recognizing your people to aim for that "spot" where they genuinely feel appreciated.

> # Appreciation can make a day, even change a life. Your willingness to put it into words is all that is neccessary.

MARGARET COUSINS

When thinking about this feeling of being appreciated, here are four outcomes that you should be striving for from the person who you're recognizing:

- **Feeling valued** – Feeling valued through recognition helps us feel good about ourselves, reinforcing a positive sense of self-worth. A survey from the American Psychological Association found that feeling valued at work was linked to better physical and mental health, as well as higher levels of engagement, satisfaction and motivation[23].

- **Feeling seen** – Feeling seen and being noticed by others through recognition makes us feel that we're important to others. Studies have found that being seen is necessary to feel like we matter and promote mental and emotional wellbeing. Social psychologists Morris Rosenburg and Claire McCullough wrote that feeling noticed is "the most elementary form of mattering."

- **Having a sense of meaning** – Being recognized delivers a sense of meaning, showing us that the work we are doing is meaningful and that it's making a difference. The Austrian psychiatrist and Holocaust survivor, Victor Frankl, said that as human beings we are motivated by a "will to meaning."

- **Feeling connected** – And finally, recognition can help us feel connected to one another, strengthening bonds and leading to stronger and more meaningful relationships. Studies have shown that social connection can lower anxiety and depression, help us regulate our emotions, lead to higher self-esteem and empathy, and actually improve our immune systems.

Let me end by explaining the exclamation mark, which you may have noticed was at the end of the words "Appreciate it!" This was done intentionally to leverage the power of an exclamation point, informally known as a bang or a shriek, which is used in a phrase or sentence to create a strong meaning, emphasis or feeling.

This is exactly what you need to do with your recognition, create that feeling of appreciation that ends with an exclamation point, with that bang! If you think of this as you recite the mantra to yourself, it will help you move to this outcome, moving from good to great, from ordinary to extraordinary. Do this and you're well on your way to having a team of superheroes as we talked about in the last chapter, who can work with you to achieve amazing results!

Calls to action:

- Rate yourself on how well you are currently doing for each of the elements of the mantra "See it. Say it. Appreciate it!" Are you doing it great, OK or poorly at the moment?

See it:
Say it:
Appreciate it!:

- Jot down some preliminary ideas on what you could do to improve how you do each of these elements:

See it:
Say it:
Appreciate it!:

CHAPTER 3:
Your Recognition Toolkit

CHAPTER OBJECTIVES

In this chapter we'll cover:

- The difference between formal and informal recognition.

- Five categories of informal recognition tools that you can pick and choose to help recognize your people.

- Three things to keep in mind as you select the most appropriate recognition tool(s).

We all have toolkits, in a literal sense, whether it's a box of screwdrivers and wrenches to help us build and repair our house or car, or a group of the things we need to maintain our garden, or even cook lovely meals. What they all have in common is that they're filled with a variety of items that have different functions and purposes that help us perform at our best.

The same is true with recognition, where a toolkit is required to help you recognize your people in a variety of ways based on what they've done, and how they like and need to be recognized. If you only have one tool, or one way of recognizing, it would be like using a hammer or a spatula to do every task, no matter what it called for!

By having multiple recognition tools, you have the flexibility to recognize your people based on individual contributions (what they've done) and individual preferences (how they want and need to feel appreciated). This helps connect and recognize your people in more meaningful and lasting ways while making sure that recognition doesn't become boring and expected.

"Having more than one card to play will make sure people are hearing the appreciation versus letting it fade into the background," says Alex Powell, Director of Client Cultural Insights, Reward Gateway.

But with all of these tools available, it's important to be familiar with what they are and when and how to use them, so you can use your recognition tools in the most effective ways. If you don't do this, you'll end up in a situation similar to where I am when it comes to my garden tools, which is with most of them lying broken in my shed because I've used them in the wrong way!

Recognition tools are normally separated into two main categories – formal and informal. Formal recognition tools are the ones that are developed and governed by specific rules and processes that your company has established, and are most often used across the entire business. Common ones include programs such as employee of the year or month, long service awards, and digital e-Cards or postcards. Since they differ from company to company, it's not worth going into detail for this guide, but I highly encourage you to familiarize yourself with any formal recognition tools your company has established. Most importantly, understand why, when and how to use them effectively in combination with the informal recognition tools described below. Whether that's by going to your manager or your Human Resources team, it's important to understand all of the tools available in your toolkit.

> If you're looking for ideas or inspiration for formal recognition programs at your company, go to Appendix 1. Here I've shared examples that I've taken from my book titled *Appreciate it! The Playbook for Employee Recognition*.

> " We make a living by what we get, but we make a life by what we give. "

WINSTON CHURCHILL

YOUR INFORMAL RECOGNITION TOOLS

As the name implies, informal recognition tools are used in more unstructured, free-flowing ways at your discretion. These, along with your formal recognition tools, work together to recognize your people, making them feel appreciated.

In this chapter, we'll explore some of these informal recognition tools that companies use. As you look through them, keep in mind that this is just a sampling, for I could fill an entire book with all the wonderful things that companies do (and I have before!). As you select these tools, keep in mind and match them to the following:

1. **The action and behavior** – It's important to recognize at the appropriate level based on the action and behavior that has been observed. Take the time to consider the scope and impact of the *input*, the action and behavior, before you select the *output*, the tool you will ultimately use to deliver recognition. For example, if your employee has done something that impacts one colleague you may do something small, a token, but if they do something that impacts the entire team you'd do something a bit bigger. The key is to get the relationship and balance between the input and output right.

   Here's an example that highlights what happens when the balance is not right. A manager at a hospital decided to give his employees who went above and beyond to help a patient a voucher to get a free cup of coffee at a shop outside of the hospital. And although this was a lovely thing to do as it meant not having to drink coffee from a machine in the hospital, some employees felt that a cup of coffee wasn't enough based on what they did, saying "I save a life and all I get is a lousy cup of coffee."

2. **The person being recognized** – When it comes to informal recognition, there are so many ways to do it. In fact, one of the first books I read on this topic is titled *1001 Ways to*

Reward Employees. But with all of these options, it's even more important to make sure that you take the time to understand personal preferences, understanding how best the individual would feel appreciated and recognized.

For example, if someone on your team is focused on being promoted, they may appreciate something that relates to their development, like going on a training course or shadowing you in a meeting. If on the other hand, you have someone who you know loves cycling, they may appreciate having an afternoon off so they can spend a few hours on their bike.

3. **The person giving recognition** – And finally, it's important for you to recognize in ways that work for you, reflecting your personality and style. For example, as mentioned in the introduction, at a previous company one of the managers was known for recognizing his team by giving out bags of handmade cookies that he had baked. This was so personal to him, and something that in turn meant so much to those who received them, and not just because they tasted amazing. However, this may not be right for you, so find your own version of recognition "cookies" that will bring your personality (and appreciation) out!

Since there are so many different kinds of informal recognition, I've grouped them into the following five categories to create a bit of order and structure to them:

1. Growth/development opportunities
2. Gifts
3. Time
4. Activities
5. Communication

Before I go into the details for each of these, let me first make three important points to keep in mind as you select and use them.

- **Recognition does not need to cost a lot of money** – According to one study[6], 72% of employees said that a simple thank you would make them feel more motivated and help build morale. I say this because as a manager you may not have a budget for recognition, which may make you think that you won't be able to do it. Wrong! There are many ways to get recognition "right" without spending money, you just need to get creative and think outside of the box as the expression goes.

It can be as simple (and as inexpensive) as a name

During a recognition workshop with senior hotel managers I asked them to share what kind of informal recognition they were doing with their teams. One person shared that she goes out of her way to use the names of her employees when she interacts with them. By doing this it makes the employee feel valued, respected and appreciated as there are over 100 employees at her hotel, so lots of names to remember.

As Dale Carnegie said, "A person's name is to him or her the sweetest and most important sound in any language."

- **Recognition does and should NOT replace pay** – We often confuse pay, which includes elements such as salary, bonuses and commission, with recognition. And because of this, I need to clarify this important distinction. Though they all relate to your employee's performance, they're done for different but related reasons. The way I like to distinguish them is that pay is provided for specific and tangible reasons, e.g. every month you get a paycheck for fulfilling your job duties or you receive an annual bonus for hitting specified financial and performance objectives. Recognition, on the other hand, is about saying thank you to your people for exhibiting certain behaviors in the workplace, whether that be hard work, showing integrity, helping a colleague or customer, or just doing a really good job. They both have a purpose and a place, so it's important to do them both, but not use one to replace the other.

- **Recognition needs to be done fairly and consistently** – Although as previously mentioned, it's important to base your recognition on the action and behavior as well as the person being recognized, it's also important to be fair and consistent in your approach. For example, if two people on your team contributed in a similar way, you wouldn't recognize one by giving them a thank you card and another a bottle of wine, as this wouldn't be seen as fair. You could, however, give one a bottle of wine and another who may not drink a box of chocolates, for this would be considered a fair treatment of them both. Trust me, your people will compare notes and if they don't believe they've been treated fairly, the positive impacts of your recognition will not be achieved.

Category #1: Growth/development opportunities

Let's look at the first category of informal recognition, which includes growth and development opportunities. This is something I've used many times as a manager as a way to show my people that I value and appreciate them for not just one contribution, but the many contributions they have made.

> When respondents were asked how they preferred to be recognized for a significant accomplishment, a study[18] found that almost half of them (47%) would choose a new growth opportunity. This was significantly higher than a salary increase (23%), a high-performance rating (21%) or even a bonus (10%), which shows the importance employees place on their growth and development.

Understanding this, many companies have a variety of growth and development opportunities as part of their informal recognition. From sending employees to formal training classes to being able to attend or present at a meeting, to being given a mentor to shadowing their manager, companies are finding ways to use this as a recognition tool, sending the message to employees that they are valued and appreciated, and their employer is committed to supporting their growth and development.

Showing appreciation by asking for an opinion

A simple, no-cost and effective way of showing appreciation is by asking your people their opinion. It sends a message to them that you value and respect them enough to be human and ask for help, and that you trust them enough to contribute to a solution. It also helps with their development, as it gives them the opportunity to get involved with something new to them.

Category #2: Gifts

This category includes a wide variety of informal recognition tools, from company-branded merchandise to food, to anything and everything in between. When it comes to gifts, I've seen companies and individuals put their own individual mark on them, coming up with ways to show appreciation in wild and wonderful ways.

"The very process of giving a gift is a clear message that says 'I care about you.' Every employee wants to feel noticed and valued at work and when that happens, culture improves."

Gethin Nadin, Psychologist, Author, Speaker,
Chief Innovation Officer - Benefex

Earlier I shared the example of the manager who gives out home-baked cookies, and another great example is one that was told to me by Neil Piper, Chief People Officer at KFC. He explained that many people at KFC have their own informal recognition awards that they use to bring out their character and personality through recognition. One of his is something called the "Culture Vulture" award, which is a £3.99 cuddly vulture dog toy, which he gives out to people for bringing their culture to life. Love it!

Here are two other examples shared with me:

- **Chocolates** – "My boss remembered a conversation from before I even joined the business that I love a particular brand of dark chocolate. One day, after a particular project had been completed (nothing major, just a regular 'doing my job' thing), I came in to find several large bars of different flavors of this particular brand on my desk. He had also bought each individual of my team their favorite sweet treat too. It's such a small thing, but it felt really personal and unexpected." Emily Plummer, Marketing Director - Beyond Encryption

- **Hand creams** – "As a way to thank my employees for taking part in some videos and marketing promotions, I bought them little hand creams from a high-end store which had inspirational and/or thoughtful quotes on them that I had chosen with each one in mind. To this day they still bring this up as a reminder of my thanks to them. This gift was especially thoughtful as the employees were housekeepers in a healthcare setting, so were constantly washing their hands and using alcohol gels." Wendy Thomas, Organizational Development Manager - National Health Services (NHS)

Challenge coins

If you've been in the U.S. military or worked for the Defense Department, you may have heard of a "challenge coin," which was previously called a "commander's coin." They've been an American military tradition for a century, used as a way to instill pride, improve morale, reward hard work and excellence, and show appreciation.

Over the years, other businesses in the public and private sector have adopted this approach, using custom challenge coins as a source of encouragement, motivation and gratitude. I've been told by companies using them that their benefits are that they're recognizable, symbolic, portable, easy to manage and can be low cost. And to make them even more impactful, I was told that some leaders and companies even have their own secret handshake which is used to give the coin to the recipients.

I've also seen gifts used to recognize company- or project-wide achievements and contributions. For example, at one company I was known for recognizing my teams for project-related gifts to celebrate and thank everyone for being a part of the project and helping to achieve our shared results. From coffee mugs to t-shirts to candies, I used this as a way to make everyone feel valued and appreciated for their hard work (especially for having to work with me).

As you select the gifts that are right for your people, keep in mind that it doesn't need to be costly and it doesn't need to be complex. It can be as simple as giving them your manager parking spot for the week, or sending them a confetti card, or even giving them a t-shirt that has your company logo on it. The key is finding something that will make them feel appreciated and, as I'll explain in the next chapter, aligns with the contribution they have made (e.g. you don't give a big gift for a small contribution).

Category #3: Time

Another popular form of informal recognition is giving the gift of time. I tend to look at time in two ways – time off and time from/with you as their manager.

Let's first look at recognizing by giving time off, something that's become more important and more valued by our people based on the new ways of working and renewed thoughts on the importance of time in this fast-paced and challenging world. Here are a few ways to give your employees time off:

- **Ad hoc time off** – This is probably the most obvious and common way to informally recognize through time, which is when managers make ad hoc decisions to let individuals or teams go home early, come in late, etc. It shows the team that their manager recognizes the hard work they've been doing and that they are appreciated.

- **Development days** – Another thing companies do is to give time off in the form of development days, which can be done either formally or informally, and fits under the categories of both time and growth/development recognition. By doing this, it signals to their employees that they appreciate them, and want to give them the time they need to learn and develop.

- **Volunteer days** – The last example, giving time off for volunteer days, can again be done formally or informally, and can again have a powerful impact on your workforce. At a previous company, I introduced three days per year for volunteer days and was surprised and delighted by the number of people who came up to thank me for doing this, saying that it showed that we valued their commitment to supporting what was important to them, giving them the time to do so.

Paying appreciation forward

At Medway NHS Foundation Trust, one of the ways that they recognize their people is by paying it forward, using it as an opportunity to not only appreciate the employee, but also to a cause that is important to the recognition recipient. The person being recognized gets to choose the charity where employees participate in volunteer activities for the charity. Or, the recognition can be shown via a monetary donation to a charity of the recognition recipient's choice. In both situations, recognition benefits and shows appreciation to both the employee and their selected charity.

Lucy Mason, Organizational Development Manager: Apprenticeships - Medway NHS Foundation Trust

The other way to give time as a form of recognition is by giving your people **quality time from you**, showing them that they're valued by giving them your most precious resource, your time. Don't underestimate the impact that this can have on your people, showing them that although you are very busy, you value and appreciate them enough to give this important gift to them. Here are a few ways to give your employees your time:

- **Quality conversations** – It can be as simple as taking the time to have quality conversations with them. By focusing your attention on them, taking the time to talk and ask them about work and/or their personal life, it can not only make them feel that you care about them, but improve your overall trust and relationship.

- **Shared experiences** – Another way to recognize your people in a way that shows you care, and again, improve relationships is by spending time with them in some form of shared experience. From going out for a coffee to attending a meeting together, to spending an afternoon with them checking out your competitors, to something as simple as going out for a walk or run together, it shows them that they are a valued member of your team. In addition, it allows you to connect with them at a more personal level, taking your connection and relationship to another level.

- **Working together on a task** – Working together on a specific task has the added benefit of helping the person learn new ways of doing things while at the same time giving the gift of your time to help and support them. I've been surprised by how much my employees appreciate me doing this, saying things like "aren't you too busy to help me?" or "I know it's not your job, but I really appreciate your help and support with this" or "thanks so much, I learned so much working alongside you."

Category #4: Activities

The next category of informal recognition tools are activities, which, as with all your informal recognition tools, will likely vary based on your company's culture. What's nice about this is the flexibility to do these activities on an individual, team or company-wide basis. Here are just a few examples:

- **Attend an external awards ceremony** – Many organizations have formal internal recognition awards ceremonies, but in addition to this, some companies use external award ceremonies as a way to thank people for their contributions to a project and/or action. I've done this myself, where I invited the project team to attend an awards ceremony event, signaling to them that regardless of whether we win or lose the award, their contributions were valued and appreciated.

- **Act as employee advocate** – Another example, which could be considered an activity or a development opportunity, was shared with me by one company. They told me of how they recognized one of their HR Administrators for her contributions by giving her the opportunity to be a company advocate, personally contacting every new employee before they join, and welcoming them to the company. This activity "brings her joy by doing the things she really wants to do, and at the same time makes her and the new employees feel valued and appreciated," said Nick Skinner, SVP Human Resources - Abcam. After all, it's great to be known as the "face" of your company and shows how much of an example that particular employee sets.

- **Have a meal cooked by the hotel chef** – Another story shared with me was from a proud father, whose daughter was working as a housekeeper in a hotel in Scotland, and was treated to a meal cooked by the hotel's chef on Housekeeper Appreciation Day. He said that normally they were given cold food from the hotel, so this was extra special for them, especially as they wouldn't be able to afford a meal at this luxury hotel.

Involving others through recognition

"One way I recognized my team members at previous companies was by giving them the ability and opportunity to include their partners in the recognition experience, sending them both out for a dinner together. This is a nice way to involve them both, showing my employee that I appreciate them for the work they've done, and thanking their partner for putting up with the late nights required to meet the deadlines."

Paul Morgan, Director of Learning and Organizational Development - ForHousing

---

Category #5: Communication

The final category of informal recognition is communication, which refers to recognizing your people through written and verbal communication practices. Here are a few examples to bring this idea to life:

- **Handwritten notes** – Many companies use informal and ad hoc handwritten recognition notes as a way to supplement their formal recognition program. For example, one online retailer I interviewed has what they call a "Celebration Station" set up on each floor that contains recognition postcards. Any manager (or employee) can select one amongst the range of postcards, write a message, and then send it to someone as a way to informally recognize one another.

- **Shout outs** – Another effective way to communicate recognition is through something called a "shout out." In my book *Build It: The Rebel Playbook for Employee Engagement,* I shared a story about SnackNation's "Crush It Call," where every Friday at 4:00 p.m., their employees would share stories of how colleagues had "crushed it," shining a light on the accomplishments and everyday victories that might otherwise go unsung.

- **Celebration shout outs** – Another way that companies are recognizing their employees is through what I'm going to call "celebration moments." They are anything from promotions to birthdays to anniversaries to the birth of a child or buying a new house – anything and everything that you want to shout out and celebrate. This recognizes your employee's professional and personal moments to be celebrated, making them feel seen, valued and appreciated.

Let me mention that for this category, as with the others, it doesn't have to just come from you. In fact, often a message or shout out from a senior leader or even a colleague can have a completely different positive impact on your employee.

Monthly appreciation video

Working in a call center can often be a challenging place to work and to spot recognition moments. As customers tend to contact them with problems, often the great work employees do is overlooked or not appreciated for it doesn't fit the norm of what is typically recognized.

At Reward Gateway, a global HR technology company, their Support Center leadership team decided to do something about this. Focusing on their company value of "Delight Our Customer," they create a monthly video to celebrate and highlight the appreciation employees receive from customers as well as collective achievements.

"It all began with a brief video with the positive comments we received which was shared during our monthly team meeting. It was intended as a one-time thing, but the video was so well received that we've been doing it ever since. To this day, the video is the highlight of the meeting as it helps us feel a stronger connection to our customers and also among ourselves. Overall, I believe this has improved the team's perception of the importance of their work and the difference they can make to our customers. It also helps them feel that they're not alone, but a part of something much bigger, connecting them to our mission of 'Making the world a better place to work.'"

Drago Markov, Head of Employee Support - Reward Gateway

BRINGING IT ALL TOGETHER

Before ending this section, I thought I'd share two ways that I and others have brought some of these informal recognition tools together into one recognition practice. This might not be necessary in your case, but if you're curious, here are a few examples to get you on your way.

- The first is a **recognition wheel**, which many companies I've worked with and interviewed are using as a fun and interactive way to recognize their people. One company that did this is Ascentis, which is one of the U.K.'s leading educational charities. Managers can recognize employees at any time by giving them a special red celebration ticket for going above and beyond. Once they've collected three of these tickets, the employee gets to spin the winning wheel, where they can win prizes such as a day of annual leave, a treat basket, a double lunch break, cakes served in one of their themed rooms or even a secret lucky bag.

Another company that does this is Tony's Chocoloney, a maker of amazing chocolates who are based in the Netherlands. They have a "Wheel of Wonders" that employees can spin whenever they win the Tony's Award or other recognition awards. During the pandemic, they adapted it to be the "QuaranTony Wheel," that employees could spin after winning one of their many online quizzes or other virtual team activities taking place during lockdown. Some of the wheel prizes were a six-pack of Corona, toilet paper, a voucher for a visit to the hairdressers, a LEGO kit, a movie night kit and a voucher for a meal cooked by their office chef.

- The second is a **recognition deck of cards**, which I developed at two of my previous companies. The decks contain 52 cards showing different informal recognition tools that, like a deck of cards, were sorted into suits and separated into categories of low-, middle- and high-cost recognition. It was a fun way for employees to select which recognition tool would mean the most to them to make sure the recognition programs met their personal needs. Here are some examples of what was on these cards to give you a flavor of the range of them:

For individuals:

- Give them a bottle of vitamins with a note to say "thanks for the energy."
- Buy them tickets to a movie or concert.
- Give them a dedicated parking spot for a week or month.

- Take on their least favorite job for a day.
- Answer their phone, emails or online messages for the day.
- Let them have an extra 15 or 30 minutes for their break.
- Pay for a babysitter.
- Donate money to their favorite charity on their behalf.

For your team:

- Buy them all an ice cream on a hot day.
- Stop for 30 minutes and play a movie trivia game and treat everyone to popcorn and/or chocolates.
- Treat them all to pizza (or something else) for lunch.
- Create a playlist of everyone's favorite songs.
- Create a yearbook with pictures and stories of their achievements throughout the year (or month or quarter).

Calls to action:

- Write down the things that you are currently doing to informally recognize your people, and rate them as follows:
  Great - they're working really well, I'll continue doing them.
  OK - they're working fine, but I need to change them to be more effective. Poor - they don't work, and I shouldn't continue using them.

- Go back and highlight any of the informal recognition tools included in this chapter that you think would work for you and your team. Once you do this, make a list so that you can include them along with the ones you're currently doing. This is your plan for informal recognition.

- Once you have your plan for informal recognition developed from the two previous actions, determine which ones are best for each member of your team, e.g. which fits their personality, style or needs? And if you're like me and love spreadsheets, please refer to a sample one appearing in Appendix 3.

CHAPTER 4:
The Four Golden Rules of Appreciation

CHAPTER OBJECTIVES

In this chapter, we'll cover:

- An introduction to the four golden rules of appreciation, and the acronym which brings them together.

- How you can use the golden rules to create a focus to help you show appreciation through recognition.

INTRODUCTION

As explained in the last chapter, there are many tools at your fingertips that can be used to recognize your people to make them feel appreciated. However, even if you select the *right* tools, if you don't use them in the *right* ways, then you'll never get the *right* results. Going back to the gardening tool analogy, and my misfortunes with them, even when I selected the right tools at my husband's suggestion, by using them the wrong way I still broke the majority of them!

The purpose of this chapter is to introduce you to some guidelines and tips, or what I call the "four golden rules of appreciation," to help you show appreciation through recognition in the *right* ways. Think of them like an instruction manual for your recognition tools, giving you guidance to help you use them in the most effective way, getting the best out of them to get the results you want for your people and your company.

These golden rules have been developed over the years as I've learned how (and how not to) get recognition "right," and have been shared and used around the world to do the same. Though they may seem theoretical at first, they are absolutely practical and actionable and can help guide you to new ways of showing appreciation through recognition.

THE GOLDEN RULES ACRONYM

As a manager, I'm sure your brain is filled with tons of information that you need to use and refer to in order to do your job. And for this reason, I've turned the four golden rules into an acronym, thus making it easier for you to remember, and thus easier for you to action.

The acronym is "MUST," which not only creates a call to action, we "must" do this, but each letter neatly sums up key points to help you deliver on your recognition objectives.

M	U	S	T
Make recognition **Meaningful**	Make recognition **Unified**	**S**potlight your recognition	Make recognition **Timely**

In the next four chapters I'll be going into detail for each of the rules, explaining why they are important and how to use them. For now, let me share with you a high-level summary for each so that you have a glimpse into what they mean and how they work together:

- **M – Make recognition meaningful**

  The letter "M" stands for making employee recognition meaningful, and is critical to ensuring the person you are recognizing truly feels appreciated. This can be done by delivering meaning in both what you **say** (your recognition messages) and what you **do** (how you chose to recognize the person), and when getting it right it shows your employee that you have seen, value and appreciate their specific contributions.

- **U – Make recognition unified**

  The letter "U" stands for unified, and focuses on designing recognition programs that are inclusive. Recognition should never create a divide or wedge between your workforce, with the "haves" and "have nots," giving everyone an equal opportunity to be recognized and feel appreciated.

- **S – Spotlight your recognition**

  The letter "S" stands for shining a spotlight on recognition by sharing recognition with not only the recipient but with others. The benefit is that it showcases what good and great look like to your people, it multiplies the impact as others see and get involved with the recognition, and it connects your people in a positive, meaningful and uplifting way.

- **T – Make recognition timely**

  The letter "T" stands for making recognition timely, and focuses on the "'when" of recognition. The objective here is to reduce the timeframe between the moment the behavior or action happens and the moment the recognition occurs, not making your people (and the business) wait to reap the benefits that they deliver.

FOCUS AND REMAIN COMMITTED FOR THE "WIN"

Before I end this chapter and move on to explaining the four golden rules, let me share a story with you. It comes from a book written by Harriet Beveridge and Ben Hunt-Davis's book titled *Will it Make the Boat Go Faster*, which tells the story of how the British Olympic rowing team in 2000 used one single question, "Will it make the boat go faster?" to help them win a gold medal.

They asked themselves this question over and over again during the two years of training that led up to this race and to this victory. "Will spending more time on the rowing machine help the boat go faster?" Absolutely. "Will going out to the pub help the boat go faster?" Probably not.

What I love about this story is that the British team was the underdogs. In fact, if you listen to the commentator you'll hear that up until the very end of the race he expected them to crash and burn, and to lose the lead they'd maintained throughout the race. But driven by their uncompromising focus on their mission of winning gold through their commitment to their one question – "will it make the boat go faster?" - they surprised the world and won the race (and the medal!).

This story illustrates the importance of having a focus and of having a commitment to your goal. For the rowing team, it was a focus on winning an Olympic gold medal, making a commitment to doing whatever it took to make their boat go faster. As a manager, your focus should be on making your people feel appreciated, making a commitment to using the four golden rules as a way to help you achieve this. Think of them as the lens to look through in helping you make the right decisions, using them in an uncompromising way to answer your one question – "will it make my employee feel appreciated?" By doing this, you're setting yourself, your people and your company up for a win!

"

Gratitude is a powerful catalyst for happiness. It's the spark that lights a fire of joy in your soul.

"

AMY COLLETTE

CHAPTER 5:
Rule 1 – Make Recognition Meaningful

CHAPTER OBJECTIVES

In this chapter, we'll cover:

- Why it's important for recognition to be meaningful.

- How to create meaning in your recognition messages.

- How to create meaning in what you recognize.

- The importance of understanding and respecting the diverse needs of your people when making recognition meaningful.

INTRODUCTION

The first golden rule, the letter "M," is about making employee recognition **meaningful**. This is critical so that your employee truly feels recognized, and it happens when you deliver meaning in both **what you say** and **what you do** as explained in the second part of the mantra. And as you'll see as you read this section, it's not just one simple step to take to achieve this, but in a variety of actions that are, you guessed it, *meaningful*.

CREATE MEANING IN WHAT YOU SAY

The "say," which are your recognition messages, is absolutely vital to the success of a recognition moment. Saying "thanks for your help," although very nice, does little to make the person feel recognized since there's likely little to no understanding of what they've done to merit that recognition. If instead, the message says, "Thanks for coming in early to prepare and distribute materials to the team to help them understand how the new office scheduling system will work," the person knows specifically what they've done, and how they've helped you and others.

By creating meaningful recognition messages, you multiply the impact of the appreciation, taking it to an entirely new level.

Since writing these messages does not come naturally for most people, let me share with you the approach I use in my training, which is from Gregg Lederman's book *Crave*, and follows these three steps using the "AVI" approach:

Step 1:	Step 2:	Step 3:
A	**V**	**I**
Tell the **Action**	Connect to a **Value**	Share the **Impact**

1. Tell the **Action**: Describe what the person did, their behavior or action, that is worthy of being recognized. Be specific about it so that they are absolutely clear on what they've done to earn recognition.
    Example: Thank you for jumping in to help me come up with the two new marketing campaign ideas that we can present to our client.

2. Connect to a **Value:** Next, link the behavior or action to your company values or specific focus area. By doing this, it makes it clear that what the person did has made a difference in achieving a priority or goal for you and the organization, with no second-guessing.
   Example: Your actions directly align with our company value of "create magic" as the new ideas can and will certainly create magic for the client and to their audience.

3. Share the **Impact:** Last, but certainly not least, it's important to show the benefit and impact of the behavior or action that you are recognizing. As Lederman says, "By sharing the impact, you are providing another healthy dose of respect and purpose!" So don't just say "you've made a big impact," explain exactly what the impact was, why it matters, and how crucial and important their contributions have been. By connecting great work to the impact it has, you'll elevate regular recognition to the kind of story that releases those happiness chemicals!
   Example: Your ideas and suggestions had a profound impact on the client selecting us to deliver their new marketing campaign and two more to follow. This would never have happened without your contributions. Thank you, you rock!

> **"Gratitude is not just a matter of showering more 'thank-yous' and 'we think you're greats' on employees. Hardly. It is not a rote checklist item or perfunctorily high-fiving team members. For expressions of gratitude to work their magic, they must be genuine and specific."**

Leading with Gratitude – Adrian Gostick and Chester Elton

To help you craft these messages, I thought I'd share some examples of thank you phrases that I found on a website titled readerzilla.com/thank-you-messages. These can be found at the end of this book, in Appendix 2.

Pitfalls to avoid

These three "AVI" steps are fantastic, and I've seen them make a huge difference in helping to understand how to craft meaningful messages. However, if we don't avoid certain pitfalls and situations, then it doesn't matter how lovely the message is, it will still fall flat on its face. Here are three of the most common pitfalls I've encountered that I suggest that you avoid.

1. **Hollow praise** – The first pitfall is "hollow praise," which is defined as "lacking real substance, value, or meaning; insincere or false." I describe it as the "eye-rolling praise," – you know the kind, where someone reads it out in a meeting and everyone rolls their eyes because they believe it to be so untrue. For these, "silence is golden" as the expression goes, as it's better to say nothing than to give hollow praise.

2. **Comparison praise** – The next pitfall is what Achor calls "comparison-based praise," where phrases such as "the best," "the smartest" and "the funniest" are used.

    "We have been taught that we live in a survival of the fittest world, so we praise the wrong way – using comparison-based praise, we lift up one by diminishing another, creating a hierarchy," Achor said in an interview[16]. In addition, he says that it "subconsciously limits the recipient by framing their success as a new standard of achievement – and pressures that person to continue meeting the same level of success in each future endeavor."

Achor recommends avoiding comparison-based praise, instead giving authentic feedback, focusing specifically on what the person did well during a certain activity.

3. **"Piss off" praise** – The final pitfall is something I refer to as the "piss off" factor, and the best way to describe it is with a story. The situation was that six colleagues and I received the same group message to thank us for our contributions in delivering a presentation at a conference. The message was written following the three steps shared previously, which is great, but since we all contributed differently (e.g. one person had spent months researching the topic, another a week preparing the graphics, and another spent only 15 minutes giving attendees handouts as they entered the room), the result was some pissed off people as some of us felt that the thanks was hollow and not personal enough.

In these situations, it's important to take the time to recognize individuals for their individual contributions. If everyone in the group had the same action, behavior and impact, then maybe you can send a group message, but before you do this, ask yourself "will I piss anyone off by doing this?"

Kind words can be short and easy to speak, but their echoes are truly endless.

MOTHER THERESA

CREATING MEANING IN WHAT YOU RECOGNIZE

Just as important as the "say" is the "do," which I'd like to look at in two ways – what do we do to create meaning *for the employee* in how we recognize them, and how do we create meaning *for the company* by recognizing the "right" things?

Getting recognition rewards right

Let's start by looking at it from the employees' perspective. It's important not to just throw money, gifts or anything else at your employees as a way to reward recognition efforts without care and thought attached to it. Forgetting the "Say" means you'll end up with that cringe-worthy disconnect, and completely negate the positives derived from recognition.

Here are a few things to ask yourself about the depth and breadth of your person's contributions as you determine the "do," which is your recognition reward:

- Was what they did a part of their job? For example, did they complete a task or project that may be part of their job, but did it extremely well? In these situations we often think that recognition is not necessary, telling ourselves that they're just doing their job. However, consider the effort and contributions they've made, and keep in mind that a simple "thank you" costs you nothing to give, and can go a long way in making your employee feel appreciated and celebrating great work.

- Was what they did above and beyond what you would normally ask them to do, and if so, how much? For example, did it involve an extra hour of work, a few hours, a day, a week, etc.?

- How much of an impact did their contributions have? For example, did it impact one colleague or customer, a few, a department, the entire company, etc.?

One small action . . . one large impact!

An intern at a housing company noticed that some of the building managers were struggling to communicate with their Chinese-speaking customers, so she suggested that they use Google Translate on their desktop computers. The result was that the managers and customers both felt more confident and were able to work together better.

The leadership team decided to highlight this act by recognizing the intern and making a big deal about it at an annual meeting. By doing this it highlighted the impact that this simple suggestion had, encouraging others to do the same in the future.

Take all of this into consideration, creating that all-important connection between the contributions and what you do to recognize them. For example, if the contributions involved a small step above what they would normally do and had a small impact, the reward should be small. And if the contributions were far above what you would expect them to do, and the impact was large, the reward should equally be larger.

Values-based recognition

It's equally important to make sure that you create meaning in how you "do" recognition by recognizing those actions and behaviors that don't just help your employees feel appreciated but help your business achieve their objectives and success. If you don't do this, then quite frankly you're flushing the time and money you spend on recognition down the drain.

The most effective way to do this is by recognizing your employees against your company values. As I talk about in my book *Bringing Your Values Out to Play*, this does three things:

1. You **create focus**, like a dartboard, showing your employees the target they are shooting for.

2. You **signal that values are important** – putting them front and center and not hidden away in an employee handbook or on a poster hanging in the office.

3. You create **habits** by recognizing against those values, creating a feedback loop as the values and the meaning behind them become second nature to your employees.

Recognizing your people against your company values is like a live classroom experience, teaching and demonstrating what your values mean and how they look in real-time, and in the moment.

And the good news is that this translates into positives for your company as well. According to a study[19], companies with values-based recognition programs reap these benefits:

- They are two times more likely to reinforce and drive business results.

- They are four times more likely to have their employees say that they believe in their company values.

CREATE MEANING BY BEING AUTHENTIC

Getting the "say" and the "do" right is important but equally important is ensuring that your recognition is authentic, which means being real and genuine in why, when and how you recognize your people. This is paramount, as a lack of authenticity will reduce the impact, be counterproductive and undermine the feeling of appreciation that you're trying to deliver. In fact, in my experience, I've seen employees using their bulls**! sensors to see this as it is, turning what could be a positive experience into a negative one.

To bring this to life, let me share with you a story of something that happened to my daughter when she was in elementary school. They were having their end-of-the-year awards ceremony and one by one they called students up to receive awards for best in math, science, sports, etc. This went on and on, with almost every student receiving an award as there were so many categories. The final award was for kindest student, and it went to my daughter. As she sat back down after receiving this I expected her to be pleased with her achievement, however, she whispered in my ear that she was so embarrassed, that the only reason they gave her the award was because they wanted everyone to win something, so they came up with this silly award for her. This goes to show that if it isn't authentic then it's not worth the time and effort doing it.

The takeaway from this is to always ask yourself before you give recognition if it is going to be perceived as authentic or inauthentic. If it's authentic, great, go with it. And if it's inauthentic, don't necessarily give up on the idea, but consider what you can do to make it authentic or what could you say to your employee to help them understand what it would take to be recognized going forward that would tick the authentic box.

UNDERSTANDING AND RESPECTING DIFFERENCES

To end this section, I want to spend a moment addressing the importance of understanding and respecting individual differences when it comes to recognition. By doing this, it ensures that the recognition is meaningful to that person, and doesn't miss the mark as the expression goes. I highly encourage you to take the time upfront to get to know how each of your employees prefer to be recognized and rewarded, and use this knowledge and information each and every time you recognize them.

Appreciation or punishment?

I once recognized a colleague of mine who had helped me prepare a slide deck for a presentation by inviting them onto the stage to thank them in front of the 200 people in the audience. To this person, who had no problem being in the spotlight, it was the perfect way to recognize them. However, for someone who may not like being in the spotlight it would have been viewed as punishment, as it would have been such a horrible experience for them.

Another example was shared with me by psychologist Dr. Hayley Lewis, founder of HALO Psychology, who told me about a time when she worked in a corporate leadership role. One time, she recognized a member of her team, someone who she described as quiet and unassuming. "After being nominated by her peers for the monthly special recognition I'd put in place, I purchased a book voucher as I knew she liked books and wrote a card with a message thanking her. I then surprised her at her desk, along with some of her colleagues. To my surprise, she burst into tears and ran out of the office. When I was able to speak with her, she told me that although she was very grateful for the recognition, she really didn't like being the center of attention. It was a powerful lesson to me, reminding me that we need to take the time to really understand our people or we can get it very wrong. Not everyone likes a big fuss or 'song and dance' when it comes to recognition. Adapt accordingly!"

Keep this in mind as you decide how to recognize your people, making sure that it's seen as appreciation and not a punishment!

Keep in mind that there are many ways to look at diversity, whether that's nationality, culture, gender or language, to name a few. The key here is to **pause and take the time to fully understand and respect differences and then use them to deliver the most meaningful recognition to that individual.**

Calls to Action:

- Practice writing a recognition message in a meaningful way using the "AVI" approach shared at the start of this chapter.

- Spend some time talking to your people to understand their recognition needs, e.g. what does meaningful recognition look and feel like to them.

CHAPTER 6:
Rule 2 – Make Recognition Unified

CHAPTER OBJECTIVES

In this chapter, we'll cover:

- Why it's important to recognize in a unified way so that everyone is invited to the recognition "party."

- Pitfalls to avoid and tips to follow to ensure recognition is done in an inclusive manner.

- How to recognize teams to encourage and drive teamwork.

INTRODUCTION

The next golden rule, the letter "U," focuses on recognizing your people in a unified and inclusive manner. **It's important that recognition does not create a divide or wedge between your people, with the "haves" and "have nots."** Instead, recognition needs to be universal, **making it available for all to give and receive**, thus increasing your chances of creating a recognition culture and having a workforce where everyone feels appreciated.

I say this because too often we focus our recognition on certain people or groups, or put limits on who can be recognized, e.g. only one person can win employee of the month, or only people who deal with customers can be recognized. Here are some of the negative things that can happen when we do this:

1. **Feelings of exclusion** – Limiting who can be recognized often leads to others feeling excluded, creating what I mentioned earlier with the "haves" and "have nots." This goes against the grain of a unified and inclusive approach to recognition, putting up barriers and closing the door on recognition for many of your hard-working employees.

2. **Negative reactions** – It can also lead to negative reactions from those not being recognized, or as I call them, the "eye-rollers." This happens when the names are called out of those being recognized and people roll their eyes and say things to themselves or to others like, "what did they do to win, I did the exact same thing as them," or "I can't believe they're being recognized again, they're such a favorite," or even "I give up, why work so hard if I'm never recognized!"

3. **Creates more losers than winners** – Next, this can lead to your employees feeling like either a winner or a loser, with the few, your top 5-10% of employees feeling like winners and the remaining 90-95% of employees feeling like losers.

4. **Leaves out your "glue people"** – Limiting recognitions can also leave out what Eric Hutcherson, Chief People & Inclusion Officer at Universal Group, calls his "glue people." He explained that when he was at the National Basketball Association they had their stars and their glue people, who were those that held the team together. He went on to say that if we only recognized our stars, or in basketball terms, our scorers, we were completely ignoring those that make the assists or grab the rebounds or play great defense. These people, your glue people, are the ones that day after day show up and contribute to the success of your company, and if you don't recognize them will walk away and leave your star players standing alone on the "court."

5. **Reduces the power of recognition** – Finally, with fewer people being recognized it will naturally lead to fewer recognition moments which will directly impact the overall power and benefits of recognition. It's simple math!

Everyone, even Beyoncé, wants to feel noticed and appreciated

Oprah Winfrey, American television personality, actress, and entrepreneur talks about how everyone, regardless of who they are, has this need to feel noticed and appreciated.

"There's a common denominator in our human experience: We want to be validated. I've done over thirty-five thousand interviews in my career. And as soon as that camera shuts off, everyone turns to me and, in their own way, asks this question: 'Was that okay?' I've heard it from heroes and from housewives. I even heard it from Beyoncé in all of her Beyoncé-ness. We all want to know 'Did you hear me? Do you see me? Did what I say mean anything to you?'"

"

We need to practice equal opportunity recognition by looking at recognition through an inclusion lens. Make sure that everyone has equal opportunity to be noticed, appreciated and recognized.

THE MASTERCHEF APPROACH TO WINNERS AND LOSERS

So what can we do to recognize those that truly and genuinely excel and contribute at a higher level than others? How can we have winners without making everyone else feel defeated, zapped of their drive and engagement, and feeling like losers? This was a question I racked my brain trying to figure out how best to answer until I was watching *MasterChef Australia*, a show where amateur chefs battle it out week after week to be crowned the champion. And it came to me, yes they only have one winner at the end of the season, but as contestants face elimination tests and one by one leave the show as losers, they actually leave as winners. Here's how I believe they get it right:

- **There are multiple opportunities to be a winner** – Throughout the series, there are many opportunities to celebrate contestant successes and to feel like winners, such as making it to the next level or winning individual cooking competitions. In fact, throughout the series, most contestants at one point in time have this winning feeling.
  Recognition tip: Look for opportunities to recognize your employees in a multitude of ways so that everyone has the opportunity to feel appreciated for their contributions.

- **There are many ways to be a winner** – One reason why there are so many winners throughout the series is that there are multiple ways to win. Whether it's a team challenge, a skills test or an invention test, they don't just compete in one way throughout the series. This allows contestants with different skills to have the opportunity to excel and win.
  Recognition tip: Create multiple recognition plans within your overall program so that there are more opportunities to be recognized.

- **They have mini-winners** – For each cooking challenge, they don't just call out the name of the one winner but they call out and bring forward the top three winners of the challenge. By doing this, they're creating mini-winners, who feel like they've achieved something for being called forward and for having positive words being said about their dish, celebrating their successes.
  Recognition tip: Celebrate not just recognition award winners, but runner-ups and highly commended.

- **There are constant learning moments** – Throughout every challenge, contestants are given feedback from the judges, positive and negative, which helps them learn and grow as chefs. One by one as they leave the show they consistently say the same thing, which is to thank the judges for such an amazing learning experience. In the last episode I watched, the contestant said, "I feel confident in my abilities, like I can fly out the door," which sounds like a winner and not a loser to me!
  Recognition tip: Teach your employees how to give meaningful recognition so that recognition provides both appreciation and learning moments.

- **They celebrate when they are eliminated** – Although no one likes to lose and have to leave the show, they do this with such genuine respect and admiration, focusing on what they have done and not the fact that they have lost. So much so, that the final thing shared about the contestant in an episode is what they've done next to follow their cooking dream, whether that's an apprenticeship, a food blog or even if they've opened up their own line of sauces. This is how they've taken what they've learned to move forward as a winner – and not a loser.

"I believe the world is big enough that everyone can have success, and that you don't have to lose in order for me to win. We can all coexist, and all have an equal opportunity to be recognized."

Eric Hutcherson, Chief People & Inclusion
Officer, Universal Music Group

TIPS FOR RECOGNIZING IN A UNIFIED AND INCLUSIVE MANNER

Moving on to the positives and actions that you can take, here are three things to keep in mind to recognize your people in a unified and inclusive manner:

- **Look for recognition in everyone** – In the next chapter I'll be talking about the concept of seeing and looking for recognition moments, but for now let me make the point that it's important to look in all directions to find moments that are recognition-worthy. Challenge yourself to look at all of the work being done by your team and all of your people, not missing moments (and people) that may not be as visible.

- **Get others involved** – Another thing I'll be covering in the next chapter is something I call a "crowdsourcing" approach to recognition, which is when you get your people involved in spotting recognition moments. This is critical to keep in mind so you don't miss any of those important recognition moments by having your team work together to see and recognize all of the great work and contributions being made.

- **Challenge your people to take ownership** – And finally, something I always say to my employees, is that they need to take some accountability and ownership over recognition moments. I'm not saying that they have to broadcast everything they do, but they do need to make you as their manager aware of their contributions so that you can then in turn see the good and difference they are making, and if appropriate, recognize them for that, too!

RECOGNIZING IN A HYBRID WORLD

To fully drive a unified and inclusive approach to how you recognize your people is understanding the new world of work with hybrid working, the new norm for a flexible work mode. With studies such as those published in 2022 by Gallup[20] in the U.S. showing that nearly seven in 10 workers say they'd prefer to be fully remote or hybrid, it's here to stay, and we have no choice but to embrace it.

But with all of the positives of hybrid working, it also brings challenges as it means changing some of our ways of working. Once such area relates to recognition, for if not addressed it can create inequities, or as we've talked about, the "haves" and the "have nots." If you focus your recognition on those that you see in the office and ignore those that work remotely, you'll create an inequitable way of treating your people.

Now you may be thinking to yourself, how can you recognize people when you don't see them? For this answer, let's go back to the second part of the mantra I shared earlier, which is to "See it," putting on not just your 3-D glasses, but 4-D glasses to be able to see moments warranting recognition in different directions and ways. For example, when you're having your 1:1 meetings with your people, ask them to share moments they're proud of and things that they've achieved. Also ask them to do the same with respect to their colleagues, thus using the power of your collective "sight" so that you don't miss these important moments that matter and moments to be appreciated.

TEAM VERSUS INDIVIDUAL RECOGNITION

Thus far I've spoken about individual recognition, but let me end this section by addressing team-based recognition. If you want recognition to support and drive teamwork, something critical in any company, you need to find moments to recognize teams in a unified and inclusive manner. Here are four things to keep in mind as you recognize teams within your business:

- **Look for team recognition moments** – It's important to look for and consider moments when teams can and should be recognized. If you're only looking for individual moments, you'll miss the wonderful teamwork that is going on around you. Have you seen a team going above and beyond to finish a project? Brainstorm to come up with a new idea? Challenge yourself to see not just what individuals do, but what they've done (and achieved) by working together as a team.

- **Include all members of the team** – When recognizing teams, it's important that you don't miss out on anyone to avoid the"haves" and "have nots" sentiment. Take the time to understand exactly who was a part of the team, and include them all in your team recognition.

- **Consider both team and individual contributions** – However, just because you are recognizing a team, it doesn't mean that in all situations you recognize them in exactly the same way. Consider if some members did more or less than others, and if so, find ways to recognize them both collectively and individually. For example, earlier in this chapter, I shared a story where a team was recognized equally for their contributions in a presentation and where many ended up "pissed off" because of this. In this situation, I would suggest that you congratulate the entire team for working together on the presentation, and then create separate recognition messages to specifically recognize what each individual did and contributed.

- **Recognize in ways that will bring the team together** – And finally, when determining how you recognize the team, consider ways to do so in ways that bring the team together in shared experiences. For example, treat them all to a meal together, send them on an activity that they can do together, or even have them work together to present the results of the great work that they have done. Use the recognition as a way to further improve their team dynamics and build relationships. This is easier to do of course when it's your own team, but you can suggest this recognition to that team's manager as well.

Calls to Action:

- Evaluate how well you believe you are currently recognizing your employees in a unified and inclusive manner.
  Very good - I get it right most of the time.
  OK - I get it right sometimes, but it's something I need to focus more on.
  Poor - It's not something I generally consider, so going forward I need to be more intentional in how I address this important area.

- Identify ways that you can improve on how you recognize your employees, both individually and as teams, in a more unified and inclusive manner.

- Identify any obstacles (e.g. hybrid working) that may get in your way, and come up with a plan to overcome them moving forward.

CHAPTER 7:
Rule 3 – Spotlight Your Recognition

CHAPTER OBJECTIVES

> In this chapter, we'll cover:
>
> - Why it's important to put recognition under the spotlight to maximize and multiply its power.
> - Tips for how you can spotlight your recognition.

INTRODUCTION

Let's next move on to the letter "S," which stands for shining a spotlight on recognition. In the past, recognition was done in a very private way, between the sender and the receiver, but over the years we've come to see the importance of changing this to put it under the spotlight and watch the magic happen.

WHY THE SPOTLIGHT IS IMPORTANT

Let me start by sharing five reasons why putting a spotlight on recognition is important and how it can help you and your company:

1. **It helps celebrate recognition moments** – First, it's a great way to shout about and celebrate recognition moments. As a former competitive gymnast, I explain it as giving your employees the podium to stand on to celebrate and be recognized for their

achievement with all of your friends cheering you on from the stands.

And, if you're like my 20-year-old daughter, our latest generation entering the workforce, I've learned that to them, being able to showcase to others the recognition that she's received is even more important than the recognition itself.

2. **It multiplies the impact** – Another thing that happens when you put recognition under the spotlight is that it multiplies the impact of the initial recognition, or as I like to think of it, it "stirs the love around." To illustrate this, think back to a time when you posted something either professionally or personally on social media and the lovely recognition messages and reactions that followed. With each one, you got a new appreciation boost, with the impact getting bigger and lasting much longer. Because of this, instead of reaping the benefits of recognition for a few minutes, it can jump to hours if not days!

3. **It shows what good (and great) looks like** – Next, it shows others in your team what good looks like to reinforce behaviors for the recipient as well as others. If the last point said "hey, look at me," this one says "hey, look at this," as it showcases what's valued and appreciated at your company, creating both awareness and focus.

Think of it like a spotlight being used in a theater production, shining intensely on specific cast members. This does two things, it highlights their performance to help the audience's focus be placed where it needs to be, and it lights up the stage to help the performers know where to safely go and not go throughout the performance.

Putting it yet another way, as Voltaire says: "Appreciation is a wonderful thing: It makes what is excellent in others belong to us as well."

4. **It helps connect your people** – It also gives your employees the opportunity to connect in a positive, meaningful and uplifting way, both directly and indirectly. This is especially important in this new hybrid world, with the recognition spotlight connecting a remote workforce by helping them understand what everyone is working on, what they've achieved, and what everyone is doing to support one another.

    At the same time, it helps them directly connect to their fellow colleagues by getting involved with the recognition moments. Whether it's adding comments and emojis if you have a social recognition wall, or clapping and shouting out words of encouragement if the spotlight is done in person (or virtually), this involvement creates a meaningful and important connection.

5. **It encourages more frequent and continuous recognition** – And finally, in the previous chapter, I spoke about something called a ripple effect, which is when recognition is sent as a result of receiving recognition yourself. There's another kind of ripple effect that occurs when an employee sees a recognition moment through the spotlight, spurring them on to recognize someone by either being reminded of their company's recognition program or seeing a recognition moment that makes them think of something that someone else has done for them.

    This can be a powerful way to multiply the superpowers of your recognition program, having it done in a more frequent and continuous way. And since Gallup says that employee **recognition should occur more frequently, at least once every seven days**, every little bit helps!

> "The more you help people find their light, the brighter you both shine."
>
> **SHAWN ACHOR**

> **The power of storytelling**
>
> Putting recognition moments under the spotlight is a great way
> to leverage the power of storytelling. Sharing recognition stories
> emotionally connects us all, helping us understand each other better
> through the shared moment of retelling wonderful achievements.
>
> **A good recognition story makes us think and feel, speaking to us
> in ways that fancy presentations and complicated data reports
> can never do.**

HOW TO SPOTLIGHT RECOGNITION

Now that I've highlighted the reason to put recognition under the
spotlight, let me end by sharing the "how." Keep in mind that what
works with one manager and at one company may not work at
another, so like I've said all along, do what you think will work best
for you.

- **Share stories at team meetings** – A great way to share and
  showcase recognition moments is to share them during team
  meetings. You can start out your meetings this way, end this way,
  share all of the stories or some, you decide what will work best for
  you and your team. And if you want to get a bit more engagement
  and involvement, often I've rotated responsibility for reading out
  the stories between my team members, thus getting them more
  involved and aware of the great things being done.

- **Create a recognition wall** – Some companies I've worked
  with have created a wall specifically to showcase recognition
  moments. An example is one company where they created a wall
  that had every employee's photo hung up. Anyone at any time
  could write a recognition message on a Post-it and put it next to
  the person's photo for all to see and read.

- **Create a digital recognition wall** – As many companies now use digital communication tools, e.g. Slack, Teams, etc., some managers are using them as a way to showcase recognition within their team. For example, my husband did this for his team where he set up a separate channel just for recognition, where everyone could share recognition messages and stories, and where others could jump in to add emojis, like or even add their own recognition messages.

Let me end this section with a caution that goes back to the concept of diversity and inclusion. Remember that not everyone likes their recognition to go under the spotlight. So before you do this, make sure that you understand what your employee is comfortable with and what would negate the impact of recognition because of the negative impact the spotlight could create.

Calls to Action:

- Evaluate how well you believe you are currently spotlighting recognition.
  Very good - I get it right most of the time.
  OK - I get it right sometimes, but it's something I need to focus more on.
  Poor - It's not something I generally consider, so going forward I need to be more intentional in how I spotlight recognition.

- List any opportunities for you to do it better.

CHAPTER 8:
Rule 4 – Make Recognition Timely

CHAPTER OBJECTIVES

In this chapter, we'll cover:

- Why it's important to recognize frequently in a timely way.

- How to lean into "in the moment" recognition to shorten the gap between achievements and recognition moments to meet your recognition objectives.

INTRODUCTION

The last letter of the acronym is "T," which stands for making recognition timely, and focuses on the "when" of recognition. The word "timely" means to do something in an appropriate time frame, which is a bit wishy-washy, as what does "appropriate time frame" really mean? Does it mean giving recognition once a week, once a month? What, exactly, is the "appropriate time frame" to give recognition? I propose that instead, we focus the definition and our efforts on the gap, the time frame between the moment the behavior or action happens and the moment the recognition occurs.

Why wait until a certain day of the week or month to give recognition? Why not give it now before you forget, and the impact of the recognition wears off?

When I do a training class on recognition and want to make the point about timely recognition, I include a photo of my husband and me from our wedding day. I ask the audience a few questions. First, if my husband said he loved me once a year on our anniversary, do you think I would feel loved and appreciated? Next, if my husband cooked a lovely meal for us, should he have to wait until the end of the week or month to be thanked?

Obviously, the answer to these questions is **no.** I shouldn't have to wait to be told that I'm appreciated and my husband shouldn't have to wait to be thanked. Timely and continuous recognition is not just important to keep a marriage together, but a work relationship as well!

FREQUENCY MATTERS

Another element of the "when" of recognition relates to the frequency of recognition, so how often recognition is happening. According to one survey, only 25% of companies are giving *frequent* recognition, which they define as recognition given multiple times a month, meaning that **employees at almost eight out of 10 companies are not receiving frequent recognition**.

I believe this happens for two reasons:

1. **We're only recognizing big wins** – First, this is because too often we only recognize those big wins, or what I've heard called "episodic" events. The problem with this is that you miss all of those small wins along the way along with the opportunity to

recognize them, multiplying the power of recognition. As my fortune cookie said just the other day, "Two small jumps are sometimes better than one big leap."

Another way to look at this is that you are recognizing the outcome and not the process and steps you've taken to get to the win. It would be like training for a marathon and not acknowledging all of the steps and individual goals you've achieved to get you there. A tip shared with me by Ben Davies, a U.K. Fitness Consultant, is to break it down into "**non-scale victories**" (NSV) which are those small but important achievements. For example, that first run, the run you do on a rainy day so that you hit your mile goal for the week, and so on. "If you don't acknowledge and celebrate these NSVs you lose motivation, focus, and often, give up on the goal entirely," says Davies.

"It's worth remembering that it is often the small steps, not the giant leaps, that bring about the most lasting change."

Her Majesty, Queen Elizabeth II

2. **We're rationing recognition** – Secondly because people are rationing their recognition. I've seen it time and time again when managers come to me and ask – if I've recognized someone last week, is it OK to recognize them again today? My question back to them is – have they done something that should be recognized? If the answer is yes, then do it, and if the answer is no, then, well, don't do it – it's as simple as that!

Another thing to think about is that when you ration recognition, when you're stingy with it, you make it more likely that people will notice and pick apart each instance – "Why is it always them?" "Was that really good enough to be recognized?" If you use recognition regularly, people aren't as critical and can be confident that they will get their turn.

Can you ever give too much recognition?

At a conference recently I shared a story about a company where 94% of their employees had been recognized, saying what a great achievement this was. Afterward, I was asked the question, "Can you ever give too much recognition, does it get watered down if it's given too often?"

My response was yes and no. Yes, because if the recognition is not given in a meaningful way then yes, it can take away from and water down genuine recognition. And no, because as long as recognition is given in a meaningful way, then it is never too much. For example, if someone does something worth recognizing at 9:00 am and then does something different that is worth recognizing at 10:00 am, recognize them both!

As I say in my book *Build it: The Rebel Playbook for Employee Engagement*, "Recognition is not something that should be rationed; there should always be enough thanks to go around."

> **"Appreciate everything, even the ordinary. Especially the ordinary."**
>
> **PEMA CHODRON**

THE IMPORTANCE OF TIMELY RECOGNITION

So why is "in the moment" recognition important? To answer this question, let me share with you **three things that could happen if recognition does not occur**:

1. **We miss important moments** – Think of an infant. We don't just celebrate birthdays, but celebrate all of the wonderful things they do in between – first steps, first words, etc. Why do we do that? It's because these are also important moments and milestones, and ones that need to be celebrated and recognized in the moment. If we wait until their birthday, the individual moments get rolled into one, they lose their impact, and we miss the opportunity to celebrate and recognize these important achievements.

    In Deloitte's[21] *The practical magic of "thank you,"* they have a section titled "Winning isn't everything," where they share data about what people prefer to be recognized for. The highest score is for success (40%), however, it's interesting to see that 24% said it is for knowledge or expertise and 20% for effort. This says to me, and quite frankly it's no surprise, that people want to be appreciated and recognized for a variety of contributions. As they say in the report, "End results matter, but the whole process is equally important and must be recognized. Results have many other parameters, but our efforts during the process are completely ours, hence, speaks more about us."

Think of recognition like a board game - when you recognize someone they move one step forward, and if you miss the recognition moment, they move one step backward.

2. **We stifle performance** – Related to the last point, and continuing with the infant analogy, if we miss recognition

moments our infant is not encouraged to keep going after those important moments. They think to themselves, "why bother, my parents didn't notice so why should I put any effort into learning new things?"

I know I've felt this way myself when I haven't been recognized for going above and beyond to help someone or work on a project, thinking to myself, "is it worth it?" I know it sounds bad, but we're human, and as said at the start, we have basic needs to be valued and appreciated.

Timely recognition puts the foot on the accelerator

Let me ask you a question – if you were on a highway and the speed limit was 70 miles per hour, would you go this speed? The obvious answer is yes. If it was safe to do so and your car could drive that fast, of course you would, as it's what would get you to your destination the fastest.

What does this have to do with recognition? Well, if you had employees who you knew could do better and quicker work because they were recognized, would you wait to give them this power, this speed, through recognition? Of course you wouldn't, which means that by giving timely recognition your employees can put their foot on the accelerator. And, more importantly, keep their "car" – your company – driving forward.

---

3. **We lose the impact** – In my book *Build it: The Rebel Playbook for Employee Engagement*, my co-author Glenn Elliott tells the story of how in his first job he was recognized for his contributions by being told that he was being nominated for an award. He thought this was great, as it showed that he was noticed and appreciated. However, he goes on to say that it was over a year before he actually received the award, and by then he had completely forgotten why he had been nominated, and the impact was completely lost.

I've heard this happen time and time again when we make our employees wait to be recognized. I see these as wasted opportunities and in the "why bother" camp as it does little to make an impact through recognition.

Let me end this chapter with some data to bring these points to life, further helping you should you need to convince your business partners to move in this direction. The first piece of data shows that employees want continuous recognition, and the second shows the gap, as they are not getting it:

- 80% of employees[15] said they feel recognition should happen on a continuous, all-year-round basis.
- Only 41% of employees[5] said they are recognized at their preferred frequency.

The next two pieces of data show the positive impact that timely and frequent recognition has on a company, showing the difference it can make between those doing it and those who are not:

- 14% more likely[19] to have better employee engagement, productivity and customer service with timely recognition.
- 41% more likely[22] to see increased employee retention with timely recognition.

GETTING THE TIMING RIGHT

Now that I've highlighted the reason for change, let me end this section by bringing it together and sharing **three things you can do to make your recognition more timely and frequent**.

1. **Aim for "in the moment" recognition** – Practice as much as possible "in the moment" recognition, which, as I described earlier, is when there is little to no gap between the contribution

and the recognition. And if you don't have time to recognize immediately, then at least practice "in the moment" notetaking, jotting down the contributions so that you don't forget these important moments.

2. **Recognize small wins** – A key element of "in the moment" recognition is recognizing the small wins, those that work together and build up to create the big wins. Here's a lovely story from the book *Leading with Gratitude* that illustrates this concept:

   "Former Ford chief Alan Mulally explained to us that rewarding small wins shows that a leader knows what's going on. In his weekly business plan review, each member of his leadership team was expected to present a color-coded update of his or her progress toward meeting key company goals. When someone shows a red, we say, 'Thank you for that visibility.' When we work a red to a yellow, we thank everybody. Celebrations for each step show the team that it's expected behavior to make progress. People are feeling 'Wow. I'm needed. I'm supported.'"

3. **Revisit your time-based recognition programs** – If you have time-based recognition programs, which are when you recognize at certain times of the year (e.g. annually, quarterly and monthly), I'd suggest that you revisit them to better understand their "reason for being," e.g. what are you trying to achieve through these? When doing this, challenge yourself to see if there are opportunities to shorten the timeframe or remove them entirely. Ask yourself, by recognizing this way is it causing any of the problems that I've shared in this section? If it doesn't, great, but if it does, make some changes.

Calls to Action:

- Evaluate how well you believe you are currently doing timely and frequent recognition.
  Very good - I get it right most of the time.
  OK - I get it right sometimes, but it's something I need to focus more on.
  Poor - It's not something I generally consider, so going forward I need to be more intentional in how I recognize in a timely and frequent manner.

- List any opportunities you have to do it better.

CHAPTER 9:
Next Steps

CHAPTER OBJECTIVES

In this chapter we'll cover:

- Why and how to make recognition a habit, becoming a part of your "muscle memory."

- Why it's important to make recognition a team sport, adopting a crowdsourcing approach to ensure it happens in a more inclusive and effective way.

- Why and how to measure and refresh your recognition practices to ensure they continue to be meaningful and relevant.

INTRODUCTION

In this last chapter I'd like to share with you three next steps to take, and some final tips to round out what I've been sharing throughout this book. These steps, along with the recognition mantra (See it. Say it. Appreciate it!), your recognition tools and the four golden rules, will help you get ready for your ongoing quest to get recognition "right," creating a strong and flourishing recognition culture within your team and your company.

MAKE RECOGNITION A HABIT

Let's start by looking at something that is absolutely critical, which is the concept of making recognition a habit, which starts with creating rituals. We all know that something new doesn't just happen, you need to put time and effort into it so that it happens without thinking about it, thus turning it into a "habit."

There are many ways to turn something into a habit, but here are five that I've often followed, with some examples to bring them to life:

1. **Step 1 – Understand it:** Remind yourself why it is important. Making recognition part of your day-to-day all starts with a change in mindset, which comes from an awareness and understanding of the importance and power of recognition. Remind yourself that recognition helps your employees feel appreciated and valued, which is good for them, for you and the company.

2. **Step 2 – Goal it**: Set yourself goals to achieve. For this, I set a goal to spend 15 minutes twice a week to focus on giving recognition. You may want to schedule an additional 5 minutes to also read recognition, as seeing what others are doing may help you understand how to give your own recognition.

3. **Step 3 – Schedule it:** Set aside time to reach your goals so that they aren't forgotten. I lock 15 minutes in my calendar every Wednesday and Friday to give recognition, which helps me remember that doing so has a specific purpose. This could be based on your own working schedule, you may want to block in time during your lunch breaks, or at the start or end of your day. It's all about what works for you best, but the important thing is to *do it*!

4. **Step 4 – Remove it:** Remove any obstacles that could get in your way.

   For example, I make sure that I fully understand how my company's recognition program works so that it's easy to recognize during my scheduled time. During the week, I jot down any moments that I'll want to remember to recognize so that when Wednesday or Friday comes around, I'm ready to recognize and can't make an excuse of not having any great behavior to spotlight.

5. **Step 5 – Assess it:** Set aside time to review and assess the differences made as you continue your new habit.

   For example, at the end of the month, I'll look at the impact my recognition has made, such as the reactions of my employees, the impact on their work or on our team collaboration.

Creating your own recognition habits will take time, but when you get it right, you'll hit all the right notes to create your own "recognition melody" that will become a part of your everyday rhythms to find new ways to motivate your people, over and over again.

"

If you don't show
appreciation
to those that
deserve it, they'll
learn to stop
doing the things
you appreciate.

"

OYINDAMOLA ADEMOLU
(M.O.J)

A lovely story shared with me that illustrates a recognition ritual is of a leader who would put 10 pennies in his pocket, and every time he recognized someone he would move a penny from one pocket to another. This was a simple reminder to him to recognize people, keeping track of it in a very unique and effective way.

Let me end this by reiterating that there are many ways to create rituals and habits. The important point and action is to do it in your own way so that recognition becomes a part of your **muscle memory**, something that happens without you even thinking about it. When this happens, this is when the magic and melody of recognition takes place!

It takes more than 28 days to form a habit

You may have heard of something called the "28 day rule," which says that it takes from 21 to 28 days to create a new habit. I'm sorry to say, but according to a study by the University College London psychologist Phillippa Lally and her colleagues, this isn't true.

They found that on average the subjects in their study who were trying to learn new habits such as eating fruit daily or going jogging took 66 days before reporting that the behavior had become a habit. However, the good news is that the same study found that when forming a new habit, missing a day made no difference, so at least that myth isn't true.

Bottom line, forming a habit takes time and effort, but when it comes to recognition, it's well worth it!

MAKE RECOGNITION A TEAM SPORT

Let's return for a moment to making recognition unified and inclusive, which starts with looking for recognition moments in all kinds of places. To do this effectively, you can't do it alone – after all, you can't be everywhere at once! To help, let me suggest that you adopt what

I call a "crowdsourcing" approach to recognition and enlist the help of your people. It not only gives you a better chance to capture all of the recognition moments, but it also encourages your people to work together and form a collective responsibility for recognition.

When you adopt a crowdsourcing approach to recognition, you have more eyes, ears and hearts looking for and capturing recognition moments.

Think of it like a sports team, let's say basketball. If you only have the captain (you as the manager) playing the game, you have no chance at all of winning. You need everyone dribbling, passing and shooting the ball if you're going to defend your goal (retain your people), score (make your people feel appreciated) and win (drive business results). Taking it one step further, it's important to have everyone looking for recognition in all directions. Going back to basketball, it's about constantly looking forward, sideways and even backwards to see who you can pass the ball to (recognize).

How you move forward with crowdsourcing recognition is up to you, e.g. do you let everyone recognize everyone, or does that recognition need to first come through you? The key to making it work is to make sure that your team has all the facts to successfully do so. This means educating and training them on the key points from this book, e.g. why recognition is important and how to recognize to create the appreciation feeling. It also means inspiring and reminding them to look for and recognize using the four golden rules (meaningful - unified - spotlight - timely). By doing this, it ensures that they're clear on the important role they have to play when it comes to recognition, and how to do it in the most meaningful and effective way.

> **Being "positive nodes" to one another**
>
> In Shawn Achor's book *Big Potential*, he defines small potential as the "limited success you can achieve alone" and big potential as the "success you can achieve only in a virtuous cycle with others."
>
> He explains that by becoming a "positive node" in your workplace, and helping those around you "improve their creativity, their productivity, their abilities, their performance, and more, you are not only helping the group become better; you are exponentially increasing your own potential for success."
>
> This is exactly what a crowdsourcing approach to recognition does, allowing us all to be positive nodes, or what I like to think of as one another's "success cheerleaders"!

One of my favorite (and easy) ways to do this is by adding recognition to your regular meeting agendas, and having team members share recognition stories and moments. This helps give the team shared responsibility for recognition, and at the same time, it easily increases the number of moments that we remember and take time to celebrate.

"I always begin my team meetings by asking if anyone has any 'shoutouts,' sharing a story of a specific action or result that a fellow colleague has achieved. At the beginning, it was difficult to get people to share these, but as I explained to them they have to exercise the muscle of seeing people doing good things, so that over time it will get easier. This is exactly what's happened, and it's been lovely to see my team embrace recognition and look at each other differently because of this." Ken Corey, Senior Engineering Manager.

KEEP IT FRESH

And finally, as with anything, if you want something to work time and time again, it needs to continually be refreshed. Think of it like a garden, where you need to move your plants around to give them more room to grow, and add new plants to supplement the others to improve the overall appearance of your garden. The same is true with recognition, for it needs to be refreshed continually or else it'll become stagnant and lose its effectiveness. Refreshing what and how you recognize could mean anything from changing your recognition practices to removing them or even introducing new ones from time to time. Whatever you decide to do, it's important to take this step to create the recognition culture your people and business need and to meet your recognition objectives.

Here are three things to keep in mind as you refresh your recognition practices:

- **Take employee feedback seriously** – Start by listening to what your employees are saying and doing when it comes to recognition. Are there certain practices that are working and others that are not? Is one of your recognition rewards not as meaningful as it needs to be? Use your employee feedback to strategically help you meet their needs and achieve your overall objectives.

- **Measure the impact and trends** – Working alongside employee feedback is measurement, which will also help you tell if and how your recognition practices are working. For example, in looking at the number of people who have been recognized in the last month, is there one group that is being left out? Is there a dip in the overall number of people being recognized? Ask yourself, what does this data mean? Does it make sense and thus you move on, or does it tell you that something is not working and needs to be changed? Use your data to measure and then strategically react to it to drive important changes in your recognition practices.

- **Reflect on new business objectives, commitments and challenges** – As mentioned throughout this book, recognition can drive business results. For this reason, it's important to constantly keep an eye on what your team and company's business objectives and challenges are, and refresh your recognition practices to drive the behaviors and actions that will help achieve them. For example, if you're having problems related to safety, customer service, or sales, these could be addressed and overcome by creating new recognition practices to embed these actions and behaviors into your employees' daily routines. Remember that recognition is a business tool, and that you can use it over and over again to help your people and your business be successful.

Calls to Action:

- Come up with a plan for how you will turn recognition into a habit for you.

- Organize a session with your team to educate them on recognition, pulling lessons and tips from this book.

- Come up with a plan for how and when you will review and refresh your recognition practices moving forward.

Conclusion

Let me end this book the way I began, with a call to action. I encourage you to challenge yourself to take a step back and evaluate *why, what, when* and *how* you show appreciation through recognition, and take the time to build or rebuild your recognition practices to be ones that truly meet the changing needs of your people – and your business. If everyone reading this guide does this, I believe that together we can create a world where every person genuinely feels appreciated and where recognition freely and naturally flows.

And since this book is about appreciation, I didn't want to end without acknowledging and appreciating the people who have helped, supported and inspired me. This book is certainly not just my creation, but a collaborative effort from all of the wonderful people I've worked with and met over the years, and for those who were kind enough to give me their time as part of my research for this book. It's been over 20 years' worth of people, so for the benefit of you, my reader, I have not listed them all out, but know that I truly appreciate each and every one of you!

Another way of showing thanks is to pay it forward, which was actually my main reason for writing this book. After releasing my book on recognition that was intended for Human Resource leaders (*Appreciate it! The Playbook for Employee Recognition*), and receiving feedback from managers that they would love something like this to help them appreciate better, I created this version to do just that. So thank you to all of those who gave me such positive feedback on my previous book, and those who encouraged me to create this new pay-it-forward version. And thank you to my husband, Ken Corey, who not only wrote the forward from a manager's perspective but let me bounce ideas off of him as I wrote this book.

Next, a great way to show thanks and appreciation is to share with you some of the books that I've read over the years on the topic of recognition. I want to acknowledge these great books and fantastic authors in the hopes that this will help and inspire you. Here they are in alphabetical order:

- *1001 Ways to Reward Employees* by Bob Nelson
- *Bring Your Whole Self to Work* by Mike Robbins
- *Crave* by Gregg Lederman
- *Drive* by Daniel H. Pink
- *Fear Less: How to Win at Life Without Losing Yourself* by Dr Pippa Grange
- *Leading with Gratitude* by Adrian Gostick and Chester Elton
- *The 5 Languages of Appreciation in the Workplace* by Gary Chapman & Paul White
- *Think Again* by Adam Grant
- *Unleashed* by Frances Frei & Anne Morriss

And finally, let me thank you. I know how busy you are, so I appreciate you taking the time to read this book. I wish you all the best on your appreciation and recognition journey. I'd love to see and hear what you do next, so do share them with me and with others, paying it forward by inspiring and supporting one another. I know we'd all *Appreciate It!*

References

1. O.C. Tanner (2021). "Global Culture Report."

2. WorkHuman Research Institute (2016). "The ROI of Recognition in building a More Human Workplace."

3. Gallup (2016). "State of the Global Workplace."

4. Fast Company article by Connie Lin (2021). "Some Big Tech Companies May be Tapping the Brakes on the Work-from-Home-Forever Trend."

5. Achiever's (2020). "State of Recognition Report."

6. Reward Gateway (2017). "Global Recognition Report."

7. Gallup (2019). "State of the American Workplace Report."

8. Deloitte (2020). "Talent 2020 study."

9. Glint (2020). "Insights Report".

10. BetterUp Inc. (2019). "The Value of Belonging at Work: Investing in Workplace Inclusion."

11. Boston Consulting Group (2014). "The Top 10 Factors for Employee Happiness on the Job."

12. Gallup (2019). "Gallup's Perspective on Employee Burnout."

13. Gallup/Work Human (2022). "Transforming Workplaces through Recognition."

14. McCraty R, Barrios-Choplin B, Rozman D, Atkinson M, Watkins AD (1998). "The impact of a new emotional self-management program on stress, emotions, heart rate variability, DHEA and cortisol."

15. Gallup (2016). "Employee Recognition: Low Cost, High Impact."

16. Shawn Achor (2011). "The Happiness Dividend."

17. Josh Bersin (2012). "The Employee Recognition Maturity Model: A Roadmap to Strategic Recognition."

18. Thrive Global (2019). "We're Actually Praising People the Wrong Way — Here's Why."

19. Bersin by Deloitte (2014). "Employee Recognition Survey."

20. Gallup (2022). "The Four Essential Dynamics of Hybrid Work."

21. Deloitte (2019). "The Practical Magic of Thank You Study."

22. Brandon Hall Group (2019). "Rewards and Recognition Study."

23. American Psychological Association (2012). "The Stress in the Workplace Survey."

APPENDIX 1:
Formal Recognition Examples

As mentioned in Chapter 3, most companies have some kind of formal recognition program(s). In my book titled *Appreciate it! The Playbook for Employee Recognition* I detail how to design these, and share examples from over 40 different companies. To help and inspire you in case you're reviewing or updating your formal recognition program, here are a few examples taken from the book:

Celebration tickets – At Ascentis, a U.K. educational charity, managers can recognize employees at any time by giving them a special red celebration ticket for going above and beyond. Once they've collected three of these tickets, the employee gets to spin the winning wheel, where they can win prizes such as a day of annual leave, a treat basket, a double lunch break, cakes served in one of their themed rooms or even a secret lucky bag. Managers are encouraged to not only present these tickets to members of their team, but to those in other teams to encourage and support the One Team ethos.

Shout Outs from Leadership – At Charles Tyrwhitt, a British retailer, to go along with their peer-to-peer e-cards, the Company created Shout Outs from Leadership e-cards, which consist of individually designed ones for each member of the leadership group. "They are designed to reflect something funny, interesting or engaging about each leader, injecting their personality and making them appear more human. They also break down barriers and connect them to our people," says Sam Shaw, Employee Communications and Engagement Manager.

For example, the Shout Out from Phil Vickers, Director of HR, is an image of a cup of tea. "When someone had done something really well

I'd often do the small thing of making them a cup of tea and saying 'Thanks' at the same time. The e-card picked up on that and reflected something personal I was already doing. We wanted the leadership cards to feel genuine and different from the others," says Vickers.

HoxBox Surprise & Delight – At Hoxby Collective, a professional and creative services organization, members can recognize each other by sending a HoxBox, aimed at surprising and delighting one another. Whether to commemorate an anniversary, new baby or simply acknowledge a job well done, they can request that a personalized gift box be sent to a fellow member of the Hoxby community at the click of a button. "The important thing is that we own the process to ensure that each package is personalized to the recipient, because it is in those details that we show that we genuinely care and understand each other that we build the foundations for collaboration," says Lizzie Penny, Co-Founder and Joint CEO.

A Night on the Town Awards – At NextLevel, a U.S. cloud-based voice, internet and unified communication service provider, they have an award that is given for going above and beyond, or for what they describe as an effort that is "loud and proud." The awards can be given at any time by a leader, with winners being given a crisp $100 bill that they can use to go out on the town and celebrate with their family and friends. For these, it's not really about the money, it's about the experience of a celebratory moment.

Golden Wagon – At Radio Flyer, a U.S. toy company, they give out golden wagons, which are miniature replicas of one of their products, as a way to recognize one another. The wagons are passed from one employee, or what they call "Flyers", to another each month along with a handwritten "you are awesome" note. The recipient of the wagon adds their initials on the bottom of the wagon before passing it on, as yet another way to track and celebrate their achievements.

Golden Toilet Award – At Venables Bell & Partners, a U.S. marketing agency, they give out a variety of awards at their annual party, doing so in a fun and quirky way to align with their culture. An example is their golden toilet award, which is given to the employee who "takes care of shit gracefully and with class." The award is a full-size golden toilet (well, a toilet that is painted gold).

GOAT Awards – At Zappos, a U.S. online retailer, the top level of their recognition program is their GOAT Award, which stands for greatest of all time, and is an award that has been developed for the customer loyalty team. Leaders from this group each month nominate someone who has really gone above and beyond, and then together they select the person who most deserves the award. The recipient receives a life-size toy goat, a $250 gift card and is recognized in a company-wide email to share their story and celebrate their achievements.

Bobbleheads – At Atlassian, an enterprise software company, for 10 years of service, employees receive a personalized bobblehead. One copy is given to the employee, and the other is put onto the bobblehead shelf, becoming a part of the company folklore.

APPENDIX 2:
Sample Recognition Messages

Because sometimes we need a bit of help getting started when it comes to creating a recognition message, in this Appendix I've shared some examples that I found on this website: https://readerzilla.com/thank-you-messages. I've tweaked them slightly to make them more appropriate and helpful to you.

Please do not simply cut and paste these into your recognition message. Use them to inspire and get you on your way, but then personalize them based on the individual situation and your individual approach and style. Also, remember to use the "AVI" approach which was shared in Chapter 4, explaining the **A**ction, linking it to your company **V**alue or behaviors, and sharing the **I**mpact your employee has made.

Recognition message examples:

1. I wanted to take this opportunity to thank you for the effort you put in to achieve (add the action). I know it's not always easy dealing with demanding clients and deadlines, but you've been there whenever and however we needed you the most.

2. I wanted to take a moment to thank you for your work on the (add the name of project). I know it was a difficult one, but your hard work really paid off in the end. The client was thrilled with what we presented to them and that's all because of you.

3. You never cease to impress me. That was a difficult situation today (explain it), but the way you handled it with professionalism and grace was pretty amazing.

4. Your leadership skills are second to none. The way you handled things yesterday (explain what they did) was impressive to watch. I'm lucky to have you as an integral part of our team.

5. Thank you for putting in the time and effort to come up with the new ideas (explain them here) that we have just implemented. I appreciate all the hard work and effort you put into them, you are an inspiration to others.

6. You were a tremendous help in getting this project (add the name of the project) finished on time. The way you organized everyone really was something to behold. Thank you for always going above and beyond the call of duty to make things happen.

7. Thanks for all your help in making sure we got this product (add the name of the product) launched on time. Your professionalism really made all the difference in the world. I'm glad you're on our team.

8. I really appreciate the effort you've put into this project (add the name of the project). You've really been enlightening everyone with your knowledge on the subject.

APPENDIX 3:
Recognition Planning Worksheet

As explained throughout the book, you have a variety of recognition tools that you can use to recognize your people, and deliver a feeling of appreciation. To help you plan which tools you'd like to use with each member of your team, you may want to create a worksheet using a format such as the one shown below. Here are the steps to follow to populate it:

Step 1: Along the horizontal axis, list the informal recognition tools that at the end of Chapter 3 you have decided you'd like to use with your people.

Step 2: Along the vertical axis, list your employees' names.

Step 3: After speaking with your employees to understand how they like (and don't like) to be recognized, tick those that you feel will make them feel appreciated as you recognize them.

RECOGNITION PLANNING WORKSHEET

Example - for illustrative purposes only

Employees	My informal recognition tools				
	Handwritten card	Bag of cookies	Bottle of wine	Time off	Development opportunity
Employee 1	✓	✓		✓	✓
Employee 2	✓		✓	✓	✓
Employee 3	✓	✓	✓		✓
Employee 4	✓		✓	✓	✓
Employee 5	✓	✓		✓	